INDIA'S
CENTURY

INDIA'S CENTURY

KAMAL NATH

New York   Chicago   San Francisco
Lisbon   London   Madrid   Mexico City   Milan
New Delhi   San Juan   Seoul   Singapore
Sydney   Toronto

1 2 3 4 5 6 7 8 9 0   DOC/DOC   0 9 8 7

ISBN-13: 978-0-07-149729-9
MHID   0-07-149729-3

Design by Mauna Eichner and Lee Fukui

McGraw-Hill books are available at special quantity discounts to use as premiums and sales promotions, or for use in corporate training programs. For more information, please write to the Director of Special Sales, Professional Publishing, McGraw-Hill, Two Penn Plaza, New York, NY 10121-2298. Or contact your local bookstore.

The phtotgraphs for chapters 1, 2, 10, 11, 12 are courtesy of Sanjit Das; for the Introduction, courtesy of Raghu Rai; for chapter 3, courtesy of www.aiims. edu; for chapter 5, courtesy of India Brand Equity Foundation (IBEF); for chapter 6, courtesy of www.mahindra.com; and for chapter 9, courtesy of www. kanori-achem.com.

This book is printed on acid-free paper.

Contents

Preface

India's Century is not for economists, nor is it for those who are still not curious about India. It is for those who are inquisitive about India, those who have a desire to relate to this country and its people. Through this book, I have endeavored to bring the great mosaic that is India to a discerning readership.

Why India? Because it offers the rare example of a full-fledged democracy making a transition, in the span of an average citizen's lifetime, from abject poverty to an impressive economic success and a heady growth rate. The achievement has an extra dimension resulting from India's vast size and its stunning, and complex, diversity of cultures, languages, social values, and climate.

The story of India is not only about how the world's perception of India has changed, but also about how our own perception of ourselves has changed. Indians are no longer resigned to their lot, as they once were, nor are they willing to work only for a better life for their children. They'd rather have the fruits of their labor here and now, in their own lifetime. Indeed, I wouldn't have got down to writing this book if India—a land stretching from the Himalayas to the Indian Ocean—had remained frozen in time.

The India of today is experiencing not just one paradigm shift, but several paradigm shifts simultaneously. Yet some constraints remain. It is the ethos of India, exemplified by its enormous capacity for harmony and tolerance, that demonstrates the country's intrinsic character.

India offers the world a diverse set of value propositions as it walks the ramp, heralding the dawn of a new global architecture, with the world watching every step and every stitch.

Acknowledgments

I wish to thank my friend Sushil Malhotra, who left India for the United States simply too long ago but remains simply too Indian at heart, for urging me to take up the challenge and write the book after McGraw-Hill made the initial suggestion.

This book would not have been possible without the perseverance and confidence of my publisher, Herb Schaffner, who dealt with an impossible author with utmost patience and professionalism. I wish to thank Philip Ruppel, president of McGraw-Hill Professional, and the entire sales and marketing team, for their enthusiasm and support for this project.

Ravindra Badgaiyan has my gratitude for staying up long nights and helping me in my struggle to beat the deadline and finish the book.

Finally, I must thank my loving and supportive family. For almost a year, as I worked on this book, I ate into time with my family. I can never quite make it up.

Introduction: Planet India

India knows us as Midnight's Children, the generation born close to the most iconic midnight in Indian history: August 14–15, 1947, the hour India became a free nation. I did not witness the last British regiment marching out through the Gateway of India in Mumbai (or Bombay, as it was then known), but I grew up with the sounds of Empire gently fading in the background. Throughout my childhood, the British influence was visible. Almost-all-white clubs were still the social norm.

The upper echelons of business, the military, and even the civil service had a British flavor.

My sense of "them" and "us" was shaped by white neighbors; my family lived in the heart of Kolkata's (then Calcutta's) European quarter. When leaving India for "home," Europeans would put their household articles on sale. As a young boy, I was obviously inquisitive about the toys, but there were usually few offered, probably because toys were light enough to take back. The personal articles left behind were generally the heavier ones, like four-poster beds, sofas with high backs and very thick arms, and ornate candelabra with branches shaped like rosebuds. "European owners leaving/ Items on sale": to my young mind this was the earliest impression of the closure of a chapter in history.

It was a long closure, one that lasted, frankly, for decades and whatever is left will remain. India has adapted and adopted many remnants of its British legacy, as it has so much else from its past. It even made the Westminster system of democracy and first-past-the-post elections its own. There were suggestions, when the Constitution was being framed, that proportional representation of a variant of the German model might suit India's diversity better. Yet, such was the familiarity with and trust of a system that had served Britain well that the issue was soon laid to rest. There is an important message here for those who are attempting to understand India: don't look for finality, for a black/white, good/bad bipolarity. Unlike many other former colonies, India did not undertake a Cultural Revolution–like purge of the past once the colonizers went home. Instead, the new society incorporated the old: borrowed from it, took from it, reshaped it. That is why, to this day, there are many Indias, many facets to India—often even contradictory or paradoxical ones. This is a truth as important for the tourist who comes for a holiday as for the businessman who arrives to negotiate a deal.

Sometimes these memories float back, gentle reminders from old Bharat to new India. In the final week of March 2007, as India's commerce and industry minister, I inaugurated a conference on lifestyle and luxury goods. The world's finest, most exclusive jewelers, watchmakers, houseware makers, and custom suitmakers were there, talking of India being a big market for goods that were, to be honest, beyond the reach of most New Yorkers or Londoners. I was amused but not startled; this was a new India that they were talking about, an exciting consumer market. Yet there is another India, *my* India, that is rooted in a middle and lower income sensibility that is frightfully careful about how it spends its money. India, remember, is the land where more than 80 percent of disposable cigarette lighters are refilled, not thrown away; and 60 percent of shampoo is not bottled but packed in single-use packets that are priced at the equivalent of a few cents. Now India is also a market for luxury retail.

It took me years to understand the unique aspects of the nation that had been created with the passing of the colonial era. It was a very poor country, with famished beggars crowding sidewalks, railway stations, and almost everywhere else. Anyone living beyond the age of 40 was considered lucky; life expectancy at birth was even lower in 1947. Prices rose faster than income for a substantial period in free India's early history, and getting by was decidedly difficult. Every home, including ours—and we were not poor by any economist's reckoning—had ration cards issued for fixed quotas of wheat, rice and fuel, items that were not available in the open market.

Jugaad: A Form of Scientific Innovation

This was the high noon of the shortage economy. Necessity, the old cliché goes, is the mother of invention. That must make scarcity the father of innovation. India had to make do with very little, and as a result, every Indian, in his or her own way, became a master at *jugaad*, a Hindi word with pan-Indian usage that is, really, impossible to translate. It describes as nothing else does the ability to creatively "manage," to make do with quick-fix solutions. *Jugaad* developed into a survival skill for most Indians. It was the additional resource that gave greater returns within a framework of scarcity.

Every obstacle thus became an opportunity, a showcase for ingenuity. My first experience with this phenomenon was on the road to the boarding school in the Himalayan foothills where I studied. I encountered an invention that Henry Ford would probably have taken off his hat to. It was the reused chassis of a bullock cart, powered by the engine end of a motorcycle. It had a chain connecting the motorcycle's sprocket to the axle, which in turn provided the rear drive for this unique "people mover." Later I found an even more intriguing "motor car": the mating of a water pump with a jeep gearbox mounted on a flatbed plank made of locally available wood, using old tires that roughly matched one another. For fuel storage, an iron drum was good enough. There were no headlights, of course. But the owner had solved the problem by seating a young boy on the plank; the boy held a flashlight in his hand and swore furiously as other cars whizzed past.

I sometimes wonder whether *jugaad*, a form of scientific innovation, represents a suppressed Indian inventive gene. After all, ancient India is replete with the names of scientists and examples of scientific inquiry. Indians first devised the decimal system and the concept of the zero, revolutionizing mathematics, only to have their ideas taken to Europe by Arab intermediaries. More than 2,000 years ago, the medical scientist Sushruta wrote the world's first known treatise on surgery, describing 300 procedures, including the plastic and cosmetic surgery necessary for a nose job!

Around the same time, the linguist Panini wrote Ashtadhyayi, the rules of Sanskrit grammar. The highly logical, nonintuitive structure of Panini's grammar has often been compared to modern computer language. By the fifth century A.D., the mathematician-astronomer Aryabhatta had already calculated the accurate value of pi, was solving quadratic equations, and was teaching his students that the earth and other planets revolved around the sun.

Use, reuse, recycle, never throw away. This was and remains the mantra in countless Indian homes, handed down from generation to generation. So India learned to economize on scarce resources. Truck tires that were beyond retreading were first used on the wheels of bullock carts and then became the raw material for rubber slippers and sandals. No wristwatch was ever lost; in time it was reincarnated at the "watch repair shop," a countrywide street-corner presence that specialized in straightening the hands and reassembling them in a new case. Umbrellas, cooking stoves, car batteries, old radios: India had—and has—a flourishing repair industry for everything. Like the water pump doubling as a "people mover" engine, every artifact was open to multiple uses, to multi-utilitarianism. In the state of Punjab, washing machines are sometimes deployed by roadside eateries to churn butter.

Why is this assorted trivia about middle-income India relevant to the global economy? The reason is simply this: India's past tends to make it choosy about technologies and business formats it prefers. In most cases, India accepts the processes and technologies that it needs. Yet the rate, level, and chronology of their adoption are unique; India marches to its own drummer. Our past experience with scarcity determines our spending preferences. A purchase is expected to do more than just satisfy a basic need or demand.

What the world may refer to as "slow change," though we prefer to call it "careful adoption," has led to great opportunities and savings. We have jumped eras and technologies by leapfrogging over other adoption models. Take basic telephony. The landline, so common elsewhere, was a scarce commodity in India; hence, when the cell phone became affordable, it took off, not just as a toy for the rich but as a stand-in for the old-fashioned telephones that millions of Indians could not have because of an infrastructure deficit.

Thus the pager—the intermediate-stage communication technology in the West, between fixed and mobile telephones—was almost passed over by consumers.

Similarly, India skipped the electric typewriter age almost entirely, adopting desktop computers even while mechanical typewriters remained in offices. This was because few Indians—even senior managers—were fussy about straining their fingers typing. In a land of high unemployment, there were plenty of willing fingers and plenty of manual typewriter repair stores.

India's Competitive Advantage

Idle fingers or busy hands: Indians know how to use their competitive advantage. Take the mobile vegetable seller and grocer, the chief competition for Wal-Mart and Tesco, if and when they arrive. He knows his neighborhood or business territory. He takes orders on the phone, and he has a delivery boy who will cycle down with a bag of potatoes or a pot of yogurt. The Indian concept of home delivery has been established for almost all essentials, which are available on call. New entrants may try to emulate this current system, which includes home delivery and credit for even small-value purchases. This will surely challenge the sales paradigm of a giant Wal-Mart, with its unending store shelves and relatively long distance between the outlet and the customer's residence.

Attempting to find rough and ready solutions to problems is a deeply embedded Indian trait. I have no doubt that it is the by-product of an entrepreneurial attribute that is hard-wired into the Indian psyche. *Jugaad* is, in a sense, the herald of free enterprise. Gamely, with a shrug of the shoulder, with equanimity, citizens relentlessly pursue the proverbial pot of gold at the end of the rainbow. The Indian-origin residents of Uganda were robbed of their wealth, thrown out by Idi Amin, stripped of their last jackets (literally), and put on a plane to London. These refugees—India's "boat people"—soon managed to establish a near-monopoly on corner shops in London. Today, they are spread across a variety of businesses and professions and are among the richest ethnic groups in Britain.

I am told that the secret of the Gujarati (many of the Ugandan exiles had their roots in the Indian state of Gujarat) success at establishing grocery stores was that they, the Indians, first rented a small space next to a big store, matching or sometimes beating prices, staying open longer hours, working seven days a week. There was an initial cost to pay, and much effort to keep overheads low, but the British neighbor was eventually forced to move out.

Such conditioning historically has also made India a street-smart nation, poor in cash, perhaps, but never poor in ideas and never afraid to multitask. Look at India's biggest festivals—the Kumbh Mela in Allahabad, for example, a masterpiece of multipurpose intent held every 12 years, where millions turn up for a dip in the Ganga in a ritual going back to the time when the Greeks were still worshipping Zeus. The Kumbh is a concourse of all India. Business barons arrive in their helicopters and planes; ordinary people trek for days to reach the holy river from the deep interiors of India. It is the quintessential great Indian ritual—enormous, eternal, in a sense egalitarian. Even so, not everything here is otherworldly. These religious congregations are also huge business fairs. They are filled with pilgrims from the hinterland combining prayer and devotion with retail therapy—buying clothes, getting good deals on kitchen utensils, you name it. As a friend of mine says in jest: Indians didn't discover Christmas, but they probably invented the Christmas sale.

And it is this ingenuity, this ability to create opportunity, coupled with liberalization, that has lifted the nation from the depths of poverty and put it on the world's second-fastest growth trajectory, not far behind China. In the late 1990s, when the computer-dependent West racked its brains for ways to save oceans of data from disappearing at midnight on 01/01/00 (the Y2K fear), Indian information technology (IT) firms were already readjusting the date lines on millions and millions of pages of code. This early opportunity-based engagement with Western clients was converted into a lifelong embrace: India is now the most favored offshore destination for the business enterprises of the United States and Europe. Revenues worth $32 billion were brought into India in 2006 and are expected to reach $60 billion by 2010.

In June 2007, the *Economist* magazine reported on Indian entrepreneur Krishna Ganesh's venture, TutorVista. It uses the Internet to offer unlimited tutoring to American (and British) schoolchildren for a monthly subscription of $100. It is an Indian answer to a problem in a faraway country where personal tutoring of schoolchildren is unaffordable for most parents, yet deemed necessary.

The Internet is offering India's instinctive entrepreneurship an ever-expanding platform—be it for scientific research and development (R&D), restructuring, medical diagnostics and clinical trials of drug molecules, cutting-edge research with stem cells, or nanotechnology; or, in the softer spheres, like long-distance publishing, accounting, or, as a lawyer friend tells me, "in drafting every document relevant to a litigation, except the judgment."

Call it *jugaad*, or see it as a nation wedded to derring-do. Whatever it is, it has made India very comfortable with the outside world. This outlook shows in the country's competitive, and not adversarial, attitude toward the West. There is little or no rancor, much less hate, in popular discourse. The Indian entrepreneurial spirit respects competition and salutes pioneers, so much so that the Hindi film industry is nicknamed "Bollywood," an acknowledgment of the Dream Factory in southern California. Yet we see in India a greater sense of self-belief and a confidence in homegrown enterprise. In the context of globalization; there is no paranoia about "Holly-woodization" or "McDonaldization." Indian film companies and food chains have cheerfully taken on Hollywood and McDonald's in the fight to win Indian minds, palates, and wallets.

India's resilience and its ability to assimilate ideas and technologies make it a very interesting place. But this alone may not be enough for it to lay claim to global preeminence in this century. It also has time on its side, literally. Forty percent of India—a full 440 million people—is under 18. This is India's demographic dividend: this century will be driven by the energy, risk-taking ability, open thinking, and innovation of youth.

India is also unique in its multicultural, multilinguistic, and multiethnic nationhood. In the past 60 years, India has steadfastly refused to accept any single culture or religion as its creed. It has not imposed the language of the largest segment of the population, Hindi, on the rest. In fact, the Constitution recognizes 22 national languages. It also allows the adherents of minority religions complete freedom to practice and profess, indeed to propagate, their faith. And, despite many provocations, the people of India have kept state and scripture separate in accordance with the vision of Mahatma Gandhi, the father of the nation, and Jawaharlal Nehru, the country's first prime minister. They developed a unique interpretation of secularism. In the West, secularism is generally perceived to be anti-religion; in India, secularism has been interpreted as equal respect for, and complete freedom to, all religions.

Unlike other multiethnic democracies, which look at nation building as a melting-pot experiment, attempting to create a monochromatic soup with a single taste, India remains the world's truly democratic "salad bowl," with a bewildering variety of colors and tastes, each ingredient retaining its distinctiveness and imparting a different but unique flavor. It is a model of social coexistence that Europe, which exported to us the notion of modern democracy, is now trying to import. Modern India is in many ways a construct of Europe; it would be appropriate if postmodern Europe sought the perfect mix of political unity and cultural diversity that India has already found.

India represents the unique combination of a young nation and an ancient civilization, embracing economic globalization in a context that is open and democratic. This is what makes India an emerging giant and a magnet for investments.

Chapter 1

Here and Now

"India, that is Bharat, shall be a Union of States," says the very first article of the Constitution of India.

I have always found the short phrase "that is" somewhat intriguing. The two entities, India and Bharat, though spatially coextensive, are very far apart—and very different. Like chalk and cheese. Or like a leafy street in New Delhi, the capital of India, and my parliamentary constituency of Chhindwara, a nowhere place of forests and plantations set amid the low hills of central India, deep in the state of Madhya Pradesh. The geographical distance of about 1,000 kilometers (621 miles) between the two places is just a short hop compared to the vast cultural chasm.

Back in 1979, my party, the Indian National Congress, decided to nominate me to represent my district, Chhindwara, in Parliament. Political parties in India are famous, as much now as they were then, for their abundant supply of self-styled election experts. One of them told me, "You will be lucky not to lose your deposit money; you are too young to be accepted by the voters."

This so-called expert was off the mark not only for that first election, but for the 27 years that I have been in Parliament. I am not sure if that in-house electoral fortune teller is still in business. If he is, he will be shocked to find me not only still representing that constituency but having modulated my pitch over the years. In my first election, I told the voters that they needed a young person; now, I find myself telling them that they need a mature person!

My relationship with Chhindwara is more than just a long-standing Member of Parliament (MP)-constituency equation. For me, it has been a real-world university, one that is constantly up-grading my skills and updating the lessons learned, often without a conscious effort on my part. Unlike constituencies in Europe and America, parliamentary constituencies in India are vast. Chhindwara is spread over almost 12,000 square kilometers (4,633 square miles). It includes some 2,000 villages and 12 municipalities. Its population in 1980, when I first became its MP, was already well over a million, and the number has almost doubled in these intervening years. For me, when I contested my first election, it was a different world altogether. I have learned a lot from the changes in the landscape and the mindscape of Chhindwara over the years.

Having been born into an affluent family, been educated at India's premier boarding school, and graduated from the Jesuit-run St. Xavier's College in Kolkata, mine had been a privileged existence, somewhat insulated from the harsh realities of the "other" India. I had had little exposure to or direct experience of the indigence, the desperation, and the utter helplessness that defined my district. In 1979, more than three-fourths of the people in Chhindwara lived below the "poverty line," but even poverty was not of uniform dimensions. People in towns were usually better off. A third of the population comprised aboriginal tribes, and the poorest of them lived in remote and scattered hill settlements. Literacy was abysmally low. Very few of my would-be voters were literate, so election campaign literature was wasted on most of them. Only a few hundred of the 2,000 villages were electrified. Almost none of the households had access to safe drinking water. There was practically no irrigation. The few patches of wheat and paddy were not even enough for the individual farmers' subsistence. The more enterprising farmers grew oranges and cotton in the black soil of the area. But the roads were so few and so bad that a substantial part of the orange crop rotted in the village market. And by the time the fluffy and snowy bales of cotton could find a slow ox cart to carry them to the ginnery, prices had, at times, fallen too low to cover even the cartage charges.

Software matched hardware. Fatalism reigned; Chhindwara's people had lost the battle in their minds. They were dispirited and resigned to the immutable cycle of life and death within a radius of, say, 50 kilometers (31.1 miles). Most of my first batch of campaign workers hadn't even traveled to Nagpur, the nearest big city, which is about 120 kilometers (71.6 miles) away. Primary schools and health-care facilities were few and far between.

Chhindwara had total absence of electricity in rural life. At sundown, not one electric lightbulb lit up the average village. Even an oil lamp was a luxury, and a battery-operated flashlight was decidedly ostentatious. I remember villagers coming out in droves to see my rather road-worn campaign Jeep, marveling as if it were an unidentified flying object. In Chhindwara, anything that moved had high curiosity value.

In my first election campaign in 1979, I specifically avoided referring to the obvious issues like democracy and constitutional rights, which were then being hotly debated in the salons of New Delhi and Mumbai. Instead, given Chhindwara's prevailing scarcity, I stressed the basic needs and deficiencies, like the need for electricity, health centers, and drinking water. I was particularly vocal about my plan to help farmers diversify into soybeans, since this crop needs very little water and could be consumed locally to fight the protein deficiency among children. Rather than making an emotional pitch, my idea was to provoke the people, to get them to think, become curious, and aspire. I ended every speech with the words, "Let there be a new enlightenment; your vote can wait."

I knew I had struck a chord with the voters. And I did win. But with the victory came a far greater responsibility—that of commitment. It was the start of a long relationship. I realized early that people were no longer immune to change, but would accept it only after careful consideration. And of course my constituency is a microcosm of the larger changes sweeping through rural India. For example, in the 1980s, my constituents' aspirations were limited to having a permanent source of irrigation for farms, drinking water, basic education, and health care. Today, the youngsters in Chhindwara town aspire to shop at a modern store in their neighborhood and to have the opportunity to get a white-collar job and compete with their urban counterparts. Though horizons have shifted, the yardstick for electability hasn't. The voters of today remain as shrewd a judge of their elected representatives as their fathers were. They are ready to place their trust in someone who will not only inspire them to dream but also make those dreams work. This trust has remained unshaken over time, with generations of voters. My relationship with Chhindwara is now more a way of life. To the astute electorate of the world's largest democracy, politics is a game of tough bargaining. And the candidate who thinks he can shortchange his voters is truly very naive. These were among the first lessons I learned in public life.

The first signs of change came in the 1980s, when a sales outlet of the Bajaj scooter company opened in the town. It brought speed into the sedate life of Chhindwara, literally and otherwise. It also left its mark on the style of election campaigning, with the zonal election managers now being capable of organizing multiple rallies in a single day. In the December 1984 national election campaign, I addressed more than twice as many meetings as in my first election campaign in 1980, primarily because of the enhanced mobility of the election managers. Almost overnight, the bicycle ceased to be an aspirational acquisition. And more changes were in the offing. In the elections in 1989, long processions of scooters and motorcycles followed my Jeep in interior villages.

Gradually, but very slowly, incomes in Chhindwara rose. This translated into a growing demand for goods and services. A collection of ordinary indigent people was transformed into a band of astute entrepreneurs. In what used to be vacant lots in the town, rows upon rows of shops sprang up, including public telephone booths for long-distance calls, the occasional basic computer-training center, and, recently, even the first beauty parlor.

And another significant novelty was yet to appear: water storage tanks, cast in concrete. The tanks were filled with water pumped up from underground aquifers. Such technology-led changes had an unexpected consequence for Chhindwara's matrimonial market. An incident from my early days as an MP still leaves me smiling. I was touring a part of my constituency that borders the state of Maharashtra. A delegation of elderly people met me and lamented that they could not get their sons married. I was confounded by the notion that one of the duties of an MP might be to arrange suitable matches for eligible bachelors in rural areas! I did not know how to react at first, but, collecting my wits, I delicately inquired about what kind of brides they had in mind for their sons. "There's no problem with the brides," they told me. "It's just that we have been in the throes of such a severe water crisis for so many years that no girl is willing to marry into our villages, because she would have to walk 4 kilometers (2.49 miles) every day fetching pitchers of water!" The spread of water storage tanks soon reduced the number of disgruntled grooms-to-be.

By the late 1980s, there was also a discernible change in evening life. Silence and darkness were gradually replaced. One of my enduring achievements as MP, which gave me immense satisfaction and pride, was that Chhindwara could get electricity to all its 2,000 villages by 1988, the first district in my state, Madhya Pradesh, to have achieved this. Soon black-and-white television at the village community hall gave way to a color television for community viewing. In the next five years, the era of color TV had arrived. It added a penumbral glow to the surrounding darkness.

The story of Chhindwara's transformation mirrors India's rise. It captures the process of change at the lowest level. This change is none too dramatic, nor does it involve a sudden shift in the landscape, with new cities being placed smack in the middle of wilderness. Instead, Indian villages are gradually being drawn closer and closer into the market economy. And this is happening by bringing public goods and services—the telephone, broadband, satellite television, surfaced roads, motor vehicles, responsive local government, primary health care, increasing school enrollment of children, especially of girls, and above all, a greater sense of self-respect and empowerment for those at the bottom of India's age-old caste hierarchy—into places where they had never existed.

Here, democracy has acted as the social analogue of the free market. It has created a level playing field for groups, communities, and individuals who, just 50 years ago, were at the two ends of the great Indian totem pole. From *gram panchayat* (elected village councils) to the national Parliament, India has approximately 4 million elected representatives. This creates a mystifyingly complex matrix of accountability, of managing expectations, of building grassroots coalitions to deliver utilities. It makes democracy in India highly demanding. The unending sequence of elections at all levels—national, state, and local—gives the country a hectic "overdrive" of democracy, making governance an enormous challenge—but that is another story.

New energies—sociopolitical energies that pry open spaces and economic energies that sow the seeds of change in those spaces—are swiftly integrating India's rural areas into the mainstream. I have often called this process "rurbanization." In a country of 1.1 billion people, with 70 percent of them being rural-based, rurbanization sets the stage for explosive growth opportunities. It is the rise in spending power that has helped to nourish the spirit of adventure and enterprise in an ordinary person who hitherto had been unable to focus on anything but survival. The opportunity to think of enterprise had previously been restricted to a narrow group, the more fortunate, who had early access. The changed aspirations of a larger broad-based mass now hold the key to India's turning into a modern economic nation.

Bottom Feeders

Among contemporary business analysts, the credit for discovering the worth of the small man goes to C. K. Prahalad, a professor of Indian origin at the University of Michigan and an intellectual with stunning ideas. His book *The Fortune at the Bottom of the Pyramid* (2005) was an instant bestseller. It talks of the 4 billion people in the world living on less than $2 a day. Prahalad tells governments and donor agencies to stop thinking of these people as victims and instead find in them an army of value-demanding consumers. He says that advances in technology will push the poor into the marketplace and change the basics of entrepreneurship. The International Finance Corporation (IFC), the private-sector arm of the World Bank, and the World Resources Institute have calculated (in 2007) that although 4 billion people across the world live in poverty, those people have the purchasing power to represent a *$5 trillion* market.

Prahalad's argument has found many takers in the developing economies, where poverty is relatively easy to "manage" but difficult to eliminate. Political leadership in these countries is generally going into overdrive to bring the lowest end of the population, those who live on the fringes of the market economy, into the economic mainstream. Prahalad's theory is a useful justification for their endeavors. But not everyone believes that the poor constitute a sizable market. Some argue that the market at the bottom of the pyramid is too small, and that it offers no potential. The only way to alleviate poverty, they say, is to pull people up from the pyramid's bottom to at least its middle. And that effort calls for treating the poor as producers rather than as consumers. Until they learn to sell, it is argued, how can they buy?

My experience as a public representative of rural India and a close witness to its transformation tells me that, by virtue of their sheer numbers and rising incomes, it is the less well-off rather than the rich who are now dictating the terms of business. In every industry and every service, the growth impetus is coming from below, and the challenge the entrepreneur faces is to penetrate a teeming market of first-time users—be it for a small car, a simple mobile phone, an airplane ticket, or even shampoo. In India, the mainstay of the mortgage market over the past few years has been small apartments, not posh penthouses.

A telling snapshot of the stirrings at the bottom of the pyramid is the cell phone market. Cell phones came to India late and at an astronomical tariff. But regulation was soon put in place and entry costs were lowered, making the market competitive. From representing snob value, the mobile phone soon became India's economic leveler. Off the coasts of Kerala in south India, fishermen can call the markets to inquire about prices for the catch they are bringing in. Such utilities and practices, which have enabled those at the bottom of the pyramid to experience economic change, using affordable technology, are many.

As a result, the mobile phone has penetrated deeply into India and across all strata of society. Mobile phone adoption has been driven by the dramatic economic benefits it brings, and changes in work environments have also given it a boost. There are approximately 200 million cell phones in 2007, and the numbers are expected to double in three years. A tele-density of 50 phones per 100 people is an achievable goal for 2010 if we include the landlines. Under some payment plans, call rates have plummeted to one cent a minute. The world's biggest telecommunication company, Vodafone, has acquired an existing service provider, and has announced that its agenda is to make talking on the phone cost next to nothing—redefining, I suppose, the notion of "free speech."

Competitive service providers are even pooling their infrastructural resources to bridge the "telecom divide," or the gap between the urban and rural markets in telecom penetration. They have begun spinning off the cell towers to "network companies," which, in turn, are not charging rural customers for making calls within the short radius of a single tower. That enables the small vegetable grower to stay in touch with the wholesaler's agent nearby, at no cost, or for the operator of the midget-sized van to check for free if there are passengers in the village for his return journey to the town. There has been a drastic fall in national and international call charges as well. And this is changing the old habit of parents staying up until the late hours of the night, when rates were the lowest, to call their children living in far-off cities.

Aviation is a classic example of the churning at the lower quarter of the pyramid. With the government making it easier for private airlines to begin services, a low-cost airline boom has led to— sometimes literally—overcrowded skies, tarmacs, and airports. In some sectors and on some routes, planes are competing with trains (traditionally the mode of long-distance travel for ordinary Indians) to offer cheap fares.

As these telecom and aviation case studies bear out, the scramble for India has just begun. This is potentially the biggest prize among the emerging markets. McKinsey & Co., the U.S. consulting firm, has recently done a projection (*The "Bird of Gold": The Rise of India's Consumer Market*, 2007) that estimates that the next two decades will see a spectacular expansion of India's middle class to encompass some 583 million by 2025. For the purposes of the study, McKinsey has defined "middle class" as households with an annual income between 200,000 and 1 million Indian rupees (Rs, $5,026 and $25,132, respectively), in the year 2000. There will also be a relentless drop in the share (and number) of the have-nots—the number of households earning below Rs 90,000 ($2,262) a year is expected to drop from 54 percent to 22 percent. This process is expected to make India the world's fifth-largest consumer market by 2025. This projection is based on a rather modest expectation of trend growth rate, so it is unlikely to be a pie-in-the-sky forecast.

Besides, there is already a taste of a consumption explosion even in the backwater of my town, Chhindwara. Newly prosperous peasants who are turning their energies to trade besiege me with requests to put in a word for them with the chief executives and senior managers of car, tractor, television, garment, and cement companies to swing a local dealership or franchise outlet for them. Chhindwara town is now witnessing a sudden sprouting of car and motorcycle showrooms. The ubiquitous "cybercafe" of urban India, offering Internet browsing for a nominal fee, is now moving beyond small towns into the rural landscape. Some branded shirts are recording the same sales volumes in both cities and smaller towns, which is a dramatic shift from 10 years ago, when the rural market was assumed to be unaware of and unresponsive to brands.

The rural population, if it is to be broadly identified with the poor, is now contributing to the community a lot more than its sweat. Of the 23 percent annual increase in bank deposits in 2006–2007, the rural and semiurban branches accounted for a full fourth.

There's a lot happening at the bottom of the pyramid; they're building stepladders for a start. I experience this each time I go home to Chhindwara.

Business Instinct

Be they at the bottom of the pyramid, the middle, or the top, what comes most naturally to Indians is the ability to spot an opportunity to do business. This is a quality that some societies have, and others don't. Just having natural resources does not necessarily make a nation entrepreneurial. In fact, what economists call a "resource surfeit" can result in the largest deposits of misery, as many African and West Asian countries have found over the past centuries. While the big powers cornered their assets, they themselves remained mired in poverty. In contrast, countries that are virtually devoid of natural resources have made it to the top of the league, Japan and Singapore being prime examples.

What drives a marginal nation to become significant and to be noticed is the level of enterprise of its people and its policies. In this context, I often think of Switzerland, a country that is endowed with the bounties of nature: its lakes, valleys, and snow-laden mountains. But this small country in the heart of Europe does not grab the world's attention just because of its scenic beauty; it does so a lot more as a result of the entrepreneurship that it is famous for, be it in services like hospitality, banking, and tourism or in the precision and beauty of a Swiss watch or the astounding comprehensiveness of a Swiss Army knife. What is important is the desire to be recognized as the unquestioned leader in one's own field of competence.

India is a nation in transition. After being off the world's radar screen for too long, it is visible now. India's emerging strengths are not easily quantifiable. In essence, a billion-strong society is going through an entrepreneurship revolution.

Entrepreneurship, in the Indian context, is not confined to the classical definition, offered by Joseph Schumpeter, of being an agent of innovation and technological change. In India, entrepreneurship is a unique way of seizing the day. And it comes naturally to India's people, with little or no hesitation or self-consciousness. The Indian is an "insta-preneur," a portmanteau word for an instant entrepreneur. A village example illustrates the point. A person from my district had traveled more than 1,000 kilometers (621.4 miles) to Delhi, among other reasons, to buy a Walkman for his son. Proudly he told me that he had bought not one but five sets; the additional four were for resale to his neighbors at a reasonable markup to give him a trading margin. This was his way of raising the cost of transportation to and lodging in a distant and expensive city, and thus also covering the cost of meeting me.

The apparent entrepreneurial instinct of Indians is in no way in conflict with the country's long spiritual tradition, which has been society's anchor for centuries. The two are complementary resources that have given the average Indian a sense of timelessness and infinite patience. In business-speak, this translates into being willing to take long-term calls, sit out long gestation periods, and be calm and composed while wading through troubled times. This mental composure helps Indians to take their destiny in their own hands; when pushed to the edge, they rescue themselves, and don't wait for others to save them.

After the partition of 1947, millions of refugees from Punjab and Bengal came to the newly independent India. Many of these people had lost their homes, wealth, and businesses; indeed, they had lost their emotional and economic moorings. Yet they did not wait for government handouts; instead, they worked hard. The post-partition refugee explosion set up literally millions of little businesses: shops and restaurants, factories and trading houses. Today, the retail sector employs 40 million people and is India's largest employer after agriculture. It is worth noting that the retail sector in the capital, New Delhi, has a strong contingent of refugees and their descendants. In one generation, these people have effectively risen from rags to riches, creating wealth for themselves and jobs for others. Such inspiring stories are heard even more frequently today. These people's street-smart ways have enabled them to overcome the perceived handicaps of low literacy and low capital.

This is best exemplified in the emergence of the Mumbai *dabbawalas*, or lunch box carriers, as a full-fledged Six Sigma industry and a preferred case study in leading B-schools across the country. The business dates back to the late nineteenth century, when Mumbai's rapidly growing office-going population needed to have food cooked at home supplied at the workplace. Since then, it has grown into an enormous exercise in logistics, with the carriers transporting 175,000 lunches in aluminum boxes each working day, each labeled with its destination. Many of the people who carry the boxes on commuter trains are semiliterate. But they never err on delivery—come the city's wild monsoon or its sweltering summer heat. *Forbes* magazine recently awarded this industry a performance rating that ranks the *dabbawalas* with the likes of GE and Motorola in terms of efficiency and quality of service. The unique feature of this lunch delivery business is its low price and high performance. The box carriers rely almost entirely on the cheap and reliable train network.

Similarly in another region, just about three years ago, three unemployed young men started a business of cooking and serving lunch to the workers at a textile factory in the state of West Bengal. Within two years they had mastered the art of making healthy and nutritious meals while keeping costs low, through careful sourcing and efficient energy use in the kitchen. Starting with 300-odd plates a day in 2005, they are now serving 55,000 plates across the iron ore and limestone belt of eastern India each day, catering to the different tastes of miners and factory workers from all corners of the country.

This entrepreneurship avails itelf of and benefits from the country's unique social trait of sharing a lot of things and thus saving up capital for investment. The country, particularly its traditional heartland of small towns, is replete even today with families who have three generations living together. They share many things in common, be it the "family" refrigerator, the "family" washing machine, or the "family" bullock cart. This system of joint family sharing in India offers the necessary economic and social security and moral support to take risks.

India is a mass producer of entrepreneurs: those who are willing to take a disproportionate risk for the reward of profit. The man in the street who uses his pushcart as a mobile grocery is as daring a risk taker as the stationary, and wealthier, grocer around the corner. The pushcart grocer buys his stock of vegetables from the wholesale market, assuming an average price for the portion he'll be able to sell fresh and a lower price for the remainder that might go stale. His choice of a spot for parking the cart, and whether he moves it a few blocks up or down, is guided entirely by the risk calculation he does in his head.

His richer neighbor, the man at the fixed shop, is equally entrepreneurial, although he is looking at a different risk. Should he keep selling butter and cheese and toothpaste all his life, on margins as thin as the wafers he stocks? Or should he borrow some cash from the local bank, rent the vacant room next door, pull down the separating wall, and turn the entire space into a quick-service restaurant?

The Indian entrepreneur's mind is constantly weighing options

and assessing risks and rewards. If he is running a steam press (iron-
ing clothes) on the footpath today, you may find that he is a laun-
derer tomorrow. The typical astrologer, if he is smart, will soon
graduate to the far more lucrative business of trading in gemstones,
which, as a fortune teller, he would have prescribed for his clients
anyway. Many Indians have taken such a route to success. A syn-
dicate of private tutors in Mumbai recently made headlines when a
Western private equity firm invested $25 million (Rs 994,751,496)
in it. Many in India like to think big and are willing to put something at stake to realize their ambition.

The wave of entrepreneurship that is taking place in India has
resulted in constant new additions being made to the lists of the
top 10 entrepreneurs of the year. Quite a few of these names
wouldn't have rung a bell even five years earlier. Many of these recent empires had their origin in unassuming start-ups. "Rags to
riches" has become a routine journey in India. The late Dhirubhai
Ambani, India's iconic business figure, dreamed that he would set
up an energy company when, as a young person, he was working
as an assistant at a Shell gas station in the Gulf of Aden. The company he founded is indeed an energy giant that is not much smaller
than his erstwhile employer and has found its place on the Fortune
500 list. Such instances of climbing up the entrepreneurial chain
are in evidence all over. Azeem Premji, who started Wipro Systems,
a leading IT company based in Bangalore, was in the business of
Vanaspati (edible oil) in the 1970s. Hero Honda, a leading motorcycle manufacturer and exporter had a humble beginning as a
maker of bicycles.

India's latent entrepreneurial genius did not find full expression
in the colonial period or, later, in the period when the economy was
under state control. It has been unleashed in an atmosphere that
rewards risk taking, adventure, and creativity. A touching tale of
the Indian urge to take risk is the story of a young graduate from

the Indian Institute of Management (IIM) Ahmedabad, the Indian equivalent of, say, the Harvard Business School. The son of a poor family—his mother once sold *idlis* (steamed rice cakes) on the pavements of Chennai (Madras)—he refused lucrative job offers, choosing instead to start a food delivery business through which, in addition to making a profit, he wished to fulfill his life's ambition of giving employment to many poor people and thus improving their quality of life.

Is this sense of entrepreneurship recent, or is it embedded in Indians' genes? It is for economic historians to trace the origin and evolution of Indian entrepreneurship. Prior to the two centuries of subjugation under the British, and even as late as 1815, India accounted for a sixth of global industrial production, something that would have been quite impossible without domestic entrepreneurs. This skill is perhaps being manifested again after two centuries of hibernation. India is now the fourth-largest economy in purchasing power parity terms, after the United States, Japan, and China. Three of the four largest economies are Asian. This matches the relative importance of Asia in the centuries before Portuguese ships found the route to the East, before the British Navy dominated the seas, before Commodore Matthew Perry of the U.S. Navy steamed into Edo (Tokyo) harbor about 150 years ago. For Asia, it's a moment of redemption and renewal.

Across the world in one way or another, India is on people's minds. What is critical is not just the gross domestic product (GDP) weight of India as a market opportunity but the global awareness and recognition of its people, their management capability, and the innovative abilities of individual Indians. In my youth, and during my first visit to the United States as a tourist, India was an unknown universe—something vaguely conjured up by newspaper pictures of scrawny, starving bodies and, of course, the tiger, which was presumed to be roaming our streets. These images of India became ingrained in the Western mind.

The idea of India in the West has changed considerably in so very short a time. Persons of Indian origin are only 1.8 percent of Britain's population (in 2001), but they regularly constitute a tenth of the *Sunday Times*'s list of wealthiest Britons. The world's largest steelmaker, Lakshmi Mittal, is Indian and is based in London. The fifth-largest steelmaker, Ratan Tata, is also an Indian, based in Mumbai. Among the listed entrepreneurs in Silicon Valley, the mecca of information technology (IT) just outside San Francisco, Indians form the second-largest ethnic group. But long before Indians showed the appetite to snap up Western firms, they started securing contracts to conduct most of the companies' back-office functions from across the continents, with the Internet allowing them to provide the service in real time.

The outsourcing story, however, is only growing bigger. At first the jobs that migrated from the West to Bangalore, or other destinations in India, were mostly confined to call centers and software writing. But the core business was left untouched. That too is changing. For both Boeing and Airbus, the world's leading civilian aircraft makers, some critical functions that have recently moved to India include the designing of next-generation cockpits and systems to prevent midair collisions. GE's association with India began in 1902, when it installed a hydropower plant here. As recently as a decade and a half ago, it had only a few hundred employees in the country; now it has about 13,000. And these employees work in areas as diverse as health care, consumer finance, and media. Some of them are designing GE airplane engines in India, thus giving GE more value for its money. The leading investment banks are hiring Indians by the thousands to analyze U.S. stocks, a job for which Wall Street would have otherwise paid $200,000 (Rs 7,958,012) a year or more. In Mumbai, it costs a fifth of that.

While India is now seen as a country that counts, the picture was not so rosy just 15 years ago, when economic reforms began in 1991. Inflation was raging, and real GDP growth was taking too long to shift gears. The present was tense; the past seemed imperfect. Many were ready to blame Jawaharlal Nehru, India's first prime minister, for having taken the country on a state-driven, semisocialist path in the 1950s. This premise is wrong, as after independence and later, the private sector was in its infancy, resources were scarce, and poverty was endemic. Yet India was able to build a social and economic foundation from which it could one day hope to launch itself on a high-growth trajectory. Today's "India story" is being written by a generation molded by the institutions of the Nehru era—the government-incubated Indian Institutes of Technology (IITs), the medical colleges, the science faculties, and, above all, the rule of law, which alone can sponsor and nurture meritocracy. Many of the policies introduced between independence and the 1991 reform were the building blocks of the booming economy of today's India.

It is important to bear in mind that the variables for development are not just investment and policy; they depend on the "starting point" of development as well. If you start low, you cannot grow fast. The perception of India's slow development in the first four decades after independence ignores the fact that the cultural and attitudinal change that ought to have come first was missing.

An economy needs to gather sufficient momentum before it can take off. This is why there is merit in looking at the rise of India, not as a slice of history beginning in 1991, but as one rooted in a deeper legacy. This was acknowledged in November 2005 by an eminent statesman, the much admired former prime minister of Singapore, Lee Kuan Yew. He said at the Thirty-Seventh Jawaharlal Memorial Lecture:

> When I published the second volume of my memoirs in 2000, I wrote that India is a nation of unfulfilled greatness. Its potential had lain fallow, under-used. I am happy

to now revise my view—Nehru's view of India's place in the world and of India as a global player is within India's grasp.

Had these words been spoken 10 years before they actually were, they might have sounded prophetic. But in 2005, Lee was only articulating the conventional wisdom.

Chapter 2

There and Then

$\mathcal{M}$any people ask why it took India so long—almost half a century of post-independence history—to realize that change was required. Why did it not adopt a free-market framework in 1947? Why did it not see the pitfalls of nationalization and state monopolies in the 1970s? I don't always respond. It is not that there is nothing to say; it is that there is too much to say. The complexities of the past cannot be pithily summed up in *post facto* one-liners. They require a much deeper understanding of free India's early life.

On August 15, 1947, as India became a free nation, its first prime minister, Jawaharlal Nehru, delivered an iconic speech that still leaves many Indian citizens emotionally charged. It was one of history's great exhortations, a tour de force that captured the heady optimism and idealism of the moment. "Long years ago," Nehru began,

> we made a tryst with destiny, and now the time comes when we shall redeem our pledge, not wholly or in full measure, but very substantially. At the stroke of the midnight hour, when the world sleeps, India will awake to life and freedom. A moment comes, which comes but rarely in history, when we step out from the old to the new, when an age ends, and when the soul of a nation, long suppressed, finds utterance.

It was sterling prose.

Intended as a grand, inspirational narrative, the speech had no room for specific policy statements. The reference to economic goals was tangential and broad-based:

> The future beckons to us. Whither do we go and what shall be our endeavour? To bring freedom and opportunity to the common man, to the peasants and workers of India; to fight and end poverty and ignorance and disease; to build up a prosperous, democratic and progressive nation, and to create social, economic and political institutions which will ensure justice and fullness of life to every man and woman.

Yet Nehru's hopes for a fresh start and his quest to build a "just society by just means"—as he once told André Malraux, the French philosopher—were hamstrung by two issues. First, the economy he had inherited from the British had long since stopped growing.

Future historians would put the average annual per capita rate of growth between 1913 and 1946 in a band between 0.26 and –0.22 percent. In its adoption and use of technology and in its productivity, India in 1947 was not very different from where it had been in 1858, when it had come under the British crown. Overall, if the British Empire were looked at as a large business conglomerate, India was a captive market and a source of raw materials—a timber plantation or a cotton field or a coal mine. Britain housed the state-of-the-art manufacturing facilities and the corporate headquarters, not to mention the fact that all the shareholders were British. Therefore there was no surplus for investment, either by the government or by indigenous businesses. The few Indian entrepreneurs who had emerged over the previous half-century were fettered by an almost total lack of capital. The British-controlled banking and financial system had been ranged against them, offering preferential treatment to "imperial enterprise."

The second problem that Nehru faced was the absence, in the immediate postwar period, of an accepted international model of growth, or at least something that he and his team could emulate with reasonable hopes of success. It is important to appreciate the intellectual climate of the times. The idea that the free market was the best, let alone the only, arbiter of economic investment and distribution was far from accepted. Nehru came to the prime minister's office with a social democrat's heart, in sync with the post-1945 Labour government that built the welfare state in Britain. A decade earlier, Franklin Roosevelt had lifted the United States from the depths of the Depression by embarking on a massive public spending program that sought to give the economy a push. Therefore, Nehru would have liked India to industrialize (like most democratic Western European countries) under the supervision, to some degree or other, of the state.

But the central problem lay somewhere else. The democratic countries of Western Europe had not been left so utterly bereft of capital, even after a catastrophic war, as India was. None of them had a society as agrarian as India's, thus making it that much more difficult for India to bring industry to center stage. There was, of course, the Soviet model, which had converted a poor country into an industrial giant by the end of World War II, but there too there was a problem, as the state system was marked by autocracy under the supreme leader, Joseph Stalin. India couldn't have accepted such a model, as we were irrevocably committed to democracy. Finally, there was no Marshall Plan to fund and finance the reconstruction of India. Nehru and his India would have to do it alone.

A third concern, even if it may not have been realized at that point, involved the nature of the Indian state. In keeping with its broadly peaceful struggle for freedom and its orderly transition of power, independent India inherited and incorporated much of the British administrative system. This provided stability and continuity, but it also meant that India was saddled with a somewhat outmoded outlook. The men (in 1947, they were all men) who had ruled India for the British were members of the Indian Civil Service (ICS). Many of them ended up continuing in the service of the newly independent state and molding the successor Indian Administrative Service (IAS). These were stalwart people, honest and just, intellectually inquisitive and with a reputation for being fair. However, they passionately believed in and were committed to upholding the ideals of the paternalistic state.

The chief mandate of the ICS had been to preserve the colonial state, defend the (British) government's interests in India, and collect taxes. The nodal officer for each administrative unit was the district collector, so named because he literally collected revenue. It was a governing system that was designed to look after itself, not to facilitate civil society or to promote local business or free economic activity. A matrix of controls, permissions, licensing, and regulations came naturally with the system.

Nevertheless, India's first prime minister was not rigid in his methods. Nehru's quest for a growth model was consistent with his political philosophy, which made him invite varied views. In the 1950s, economists from around the world were invited to participate. Nehru, a trenchant intellectual, was the prototype of the philosopher-prince, a man in love with ideas. He had as his lieutenant a brilliant scholar, P. C. Mahalanobis, who was a statistician by training. Mahalanobis traveled to universities abroad, seeking economists and economic policymakers who were willing to help to develop a unique growth model for India. On Nehru's behalf, Mahalanobis mobilized powerful minds—Ragnar Frisch, Jan Tinbergen, Richard Stone, Joan Robinson, Oskar Lange, Richard Goodwin, and many others. Some of them were left-leaning supporters of a welfare state; others were more orthodox economists.

A minor member of one of the visiting parties was Milton Friedman. Decades later, he was to emerge as the doyen of the Chicago School, winner of the Nobel Prize in Economics in 1976, and reputedly the inspiration for Ronald Reagan's policies. When he visited India—twice, in 1955 and 1963—Friedman was still a young man. As expected, he was disappointed by the Nehruvian dream. Writing in 1963, he compared his two visits vividly:

> The roads in the countryside are notably better, there are many more bicycles and automobiles in both city and country, beggars, though still numerous, seem somewhat less ubiquitous. . . . But, unfortunately, the progress appears spotty, and some of the appearance of progress is misleading. Many of the most impressive new structures are signs not of progress but of waste. . . . As a friend from Britain remarked after his first visit to Calcutta where over a tenth of the population have no home other than the street: "One can adjust to a square mile of this

kind of thing but when it goes on square mile after square mile, it is more than one can bear."

However, Friedman's most perceptive observation was kept for the city of Ludhiana in Punjab, a medium-sized town that was fast becoming a major center for the manufacture of machine tools, bicycles, sewing machines, sports goods, and knitted woolens. Friedman was greatly excited at the sight of a "three-man shop" that assembled saddles for bicycles, with the remainder of the bicycle being made by other small units in the city. His excitement at finding a demonstrable example of division of labor was similar to that of Adam Smith. Friedman mused about Ludhiana:

> Here was the Industrial Revolution at its inception—I repeatedly felt that I was seeing in true life the descriptions of Manchester and Birmingham at the end of the 18th century as I had read in economic histories.

He ended his passionate reportage with these memorable words: "There is no shortage of enterprise, or drive, or technical skill in Ludhiana. There is rather a self-confident, strident, raw capitalism bursting at the seams."

Nehru's Options

So, what happened to the "raw capitalism" that Friedman had observed in the 1960s? It was obviously sporadic and localized, for entrepreneurship, although innate, was certainly not the defining identity of India in those early years. Perhaps it was an idea whose time had not yet come. India was not ready for it; the country was too poor, too inexperienced, too raw from the wounds of British freebooter capitalism to put its trust immediately and instinctively in the big-bang anarchy of free-market economies and of free trade. Two hundred years of British rule had, after all, begun with the arrival of the East India Company, a trading firm that had stayed on to recruit an army, then to acquire and annex territory, and finally to become the government. The "East India Company syndrome" ran deep in Indian society. The underlying dread of dependence on external forces was driving the spirit of self-reliance, and the country needed to grow on its own without being dependent on foreigners and foreign trade.

Obviously, Nehru had to be cautious. He loved his people and his country too deeply to attempt to fashion its future without caution. Some intellectuals have compared his feeling for his people to a parent's love for a child. This explains a lot of what Nehru did—like building heavy industry almost exclusively in the government sector—and why.

Actually, Nehru had very few options. Contemporary Indian big business had neither capital nor technological innovation to back it up. Without government support and protection, it would have been knocked out. A group of leading Indian businessmen had in fact been meeting since the mid-1940s, as the expectation of independence heightened, to draw up economic strategies for free India. Business barons such as J. R. D. Tata, G. D. Birla, and Sir Shri Ram held a conclave in Bombay (now Mumbai) and put together what came to be called the "Bombay Plan." Over the years, many myths have emerged about the Bombay Plan. There is an urban legend that it was a free-market, pro-enterprise charter that would have made India the mecca of Asian capitalism, but that Nehru scotched it. However, the documents of the Bombay Plan do not bear this out.

The plan used the terminology of the Industrial Age and recognized, as Nehru did, that industrialization was nonnegotiable. Yet the document was also Indian business's anticipatory prescription for protectionism. It suggested that the government should allow foreign capital to come in only as debt, not equity, arguing that there should be no threat to the (hereditary) pattern of business ownership. It urged the state to prohibit by law foreign ownership of a large swath of "key businesses," such as banking, insurance, aviation, and industries like heavy machinery and machine tools, locomotives, automobiles, aircraft, shipping, heavy chemicals, fertilizers, and minerals. Indian business groups were already established in iron and steel, cotton textiles, sugar, cement, and paper. The plan also required the state to develop infrastructure like power stations and roads, as there was very little private capital available. It is undeniable, therefore, that in India in the 1950s, there was a near consensus in favor of insulating the economy from international trade. This was deemed the best strategy in the circumstances.

And then there was the influence of Mahatma Gandhi, a colossus who dominated Indian public life and a revered father figure for the political class. The Mahatma had some definite ideas on economics, which were rooted in his practical experience and understanding of rural India. In contemporary language, Gandhi was a postmodernist, a New Age thinker who advocated simple living, eco-friendly lifestyles, and organic food. In 2007, his ideas would have made him trendy in the West. But in 1947, the same West called him anti-industry.

"India lives in her villages," said Mahatma Gandhi. He believed that a focus on agriculture was of the essence, given India's food scarcity—the 1940s had seen a debilitating famine in Bengal, killing tens of thousands—and given the fact that a vast percentage of India's people lived off the land. Hints of a subtle tussle became apparent when leading civil servants and technocrats drew a blueprint for post-independence India. The leader of this group was Sir Mokshagundam Visvesvaraya, a brilliant engineer from India's south. Visvesvaraya ended his exposition with a flourish:

"Industrialize, or perish." To this, the Mahatma's wry rebuff was: "Industrialize—and perish."

Gandhi had his reasons. He was skeptical of big government, big business, and big capitalism. He realized that the immediate need was for mass employment, and he felt that small, village-based industrial units could best use India's prodigious human capital without the need for expensive technology. This led to a "reservation" of many industries for small-scale operations, which seemed to compromise the principle of economies of scale. Toys and processed food are just two examples of industries where individual business units were not allowed to grow beyond a certain size. In many cases there were disincentives to growth in the form of higher tax rates. While this had certain social advantages, it made these businesses noncompetitive in the international market. In later years, it caused them to lose global orders to, for instance, Chinese producers, who had no such restrictions.

As the decades after independence rolled by, the Indian growth model, which had long been a matter of curiosity in the academic sphere, became some sort of a chimera. Agriculture was on the top in the first five-year plan (1951–1956), but industry replaced it in the second plan. Agriculture again dominated in the third, until India's reverses in the 1962 border war with China shifted its priorities to defense. Then there was a three-year planning gap, marked by a long spell of drought. So India was hardly remembered by the world for its contribution to the philosophy of economic growth. In the Western mind, it remained for decades the land of Gandhi, symbolized by his *charkha* (spinning wheel).

But Gandhi's ideas on economics were far ahead of his time. When the per capita energy consumption of the developing world catches up with that of the developed world, the question of sustainability will eventually hit us, and then the chiseled wisdom of the Mahatma will perhaps receive more attention.

Control's Command

By the early 1970s, India had moved from an agrarian economy to one with a solid industrial base. This period also saw the benefits of the "Green Revolution," under the prime ministry of Indira Gandhi, which resulted in India's becoming self-sufficient in food. No longer did the country have to seek food aid whenever famine, flood, or drought struck it. But the logical culmination of the early pulls and pressures, and the developmental strategy adopted, was that the state's role in the economy had grown significantly—perhaps a bit more than was necessary.

In retrospect, things seem clearer, since one has the benefit of hindsight. In 1980, when I was in Parliament for the first time, there were three fundamental elements of Indian economic policy:

1. Import substitution, as distinct from the East Asian model of export promotion

2. A controlled foreign exchange rate

3. Excessive bureaucratic control over consumption and production

While these policies are easy to criticize today, it must not be forgotten that in the first three decades of India's independence, the world was not lining up to help India, without imposing client-state conditionalities. A subtle technology-denial regime operated in the West, as it did not see India as a committed ally during the Cold War. The country was nonaligned. No one except the then Soviet Union would sell India the technology for manufacturing capital goods, lest it offer competition. But the Soviets lacked modern technology themselves; their labor-intensive manufacturing processes had already become obsolete as early as the 1960s. It was a vicious cycle.

It was the Indian import substitution model, adopted in the late 1950s, that ultimately led to the perception that trade with the rest of the world was not a priority. India wanted to develop on its own. This model allowed one Indian automobile maker, which had a technology-sharing arrangement with the Morris Company of the United Kingdom, to tweak the old Morris engine in a body that resembled a battle tank and yet have its order books full decade after decade.

While imports were tightly controlled, the official exchange rate for the rupee was overly high. This gave other Asian countries like South Korea and Thailand, which had depreciated their currencies in the 1970s, a crucial edge in merchandise exports. The inevitable happened: India's share of world exports sank.

The artificially determined, overly high exchange rate had both an economic and a social cost. It created a strong incentive for transborder smuggling of virtually everything that was in short supply locally—gold, silver, electronic goods, industrial catalysts, and bottles of Scotch whisky. The archetypal gold smuggler of the 1970s also offered an ancillary service. He helped Indian workers in, say, Dubai to remit a part of their income to their families back home at a realistic exchange rate, not the official rate posted by the Reserve Bank of India (RBI; India's central bank, the equivalent of the Bank of England or the U.S. Federal Reserve). By the early 1980s, it was at this informal (and illegal) exchange rate that most cross-border transactions were taking place.

The third overarching problem was the plethora of controls—on production, consumption, and every aspect of life, it appeared. Setting up almost any industrial unit beyond a very small size called for complex licensing. Granting of licenses, in turn, depended largely on the government officer's discretionary authority. The industrial licensing system operated in league with a host of other controls: import and export controls, price controls, control of capital issues, and control of allocation. Protective of their market, those who had licenses to build cars or two-wheelers lobbied hard to thwart competition. This situation led to the strange proliferation of waiting lists (in some cases running into years) for cars, scooters, and even some types of wristwatches. In the process, the consumer was shortchanged. This environment seems so bizarre now; it seemed so natural then. Of course, those were the days of extreme capital scarcity, and the state was obligated to allocate resources in accordance with national priorities.

Not surprisingly, between the mid-1960s and 1980, the annual rate of industrial growth averaged 4 percent. Since industry didn't grow fast enough and factories weren't set up quickly enough, most people continued to find jobs on the farm. The Indian populace remained largely agrarian.

Hard Times

The India of the Cold War years was better known by perceptions. Somebody with a sharp sense of humor once called it the world's largest democracy as well as the world's largest bureaucracy. But India did not always have the luxury of choice during those years. Natural disasters and security challenges exacted a price. In the 1960s, as India lurched from one drought to the next with floods in between and depended on food aid, a cruel critic said that the country "lived from ship to mouth." Three wars in nine years— with China in 1962 and with Pakistan in 1965 and 1971—also helped to create a sense of siege and fear of the outsider. As declassified documents now establish, in the 1971 war, fought for the liberation of Bangladesh, the United States, led by Richard Nixon and Henry Kissinger, backed Pakistan and even sent the U.S. Seventh Fleet menacingly toward Kolkata. They seemed to mock the Indian victory.

In this vitiated political atmosphere, there could not be popular support for stronger economic relations with the United States.

It took the arrival of a generation that had grown up in an independent India, along with such visible symbols of success as agricultural growth and self-sufficiency in food, to give India the
confidence and certitude to engage with the world once again. Perhaps the time required could have been shortened, but it's doubtful
that it could have been eliminated altogether. It is impossible to
delink a country's economy from its emotional well-being over the
longer term.

The psychological atmosphere prevailing in India during the
Cold War years is rather complex. Being nonaligned, India was a
camp follower of neither Moscow nor Washington. But in a then-
bipolar world, the urge to be on one's own could be indulged only
at a price. It is worth remembering an anecdote, if only to illustrate
that the Indian way—the Nehruvian way—had its takers in the
1950s. Commenting on the draft of the Second Five-Year Plan
(1956), the British scientist and intellectual J. B. S. Haldane wrote:

> Even if one is pessimistic, and allows a 15 per cent chance
> of failure through interference by the United States (via
> Pakistan or otherwise), a 10 per cent chance of interfer-
> ence by the Soviet Union and China, a 20 per cent chance
> of interference with civil service traditionalism and po-
> litical obstruction, and a five per cent chance of interfer-
> ence by Hindu traditionalism, that leaves a 50 per cent
> chance of success which will alter the whole history of
> the world for the better.

Haldane knew the India of the Nehru era well, and had assigned,
shrewdly perhaps, a somewhat higher weight to the risk of interference by the Americans than to that by the Soviet camp. Ideolog-
ically, though, India might have tilted somewhat toward the left but
never committed to either side on the biggest political discourse of
the era concerning the role of the state. Nehru was temperamen-

tally a middle-of-the-roader who preferred to either put the individual ahead of the state or, on occasion, the other way round, depending on who would deliver better. But India was too new and troubled a country for its leader to always follow his instincts. This often led to inaction. The Cold War left him cold, so to speak. Wherever he is gazing at the newly globalizing world, that grand old man, Jawaharlal Nehru, must be chuckling at the irony, and smiling approvingly at today's India.

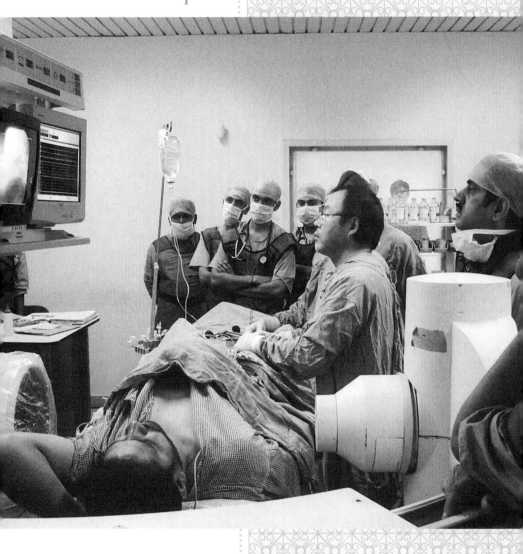

Chapter 3

Modern Times

$\mathcal{E}$very country has its "modern age," which arrives in its own time. It need not begin with fanfare. Often it is the product of crisis. It could be the result of a breach of the social contract between government and the governed over a violent taxation issue, as it was in England at the cusp of the Glorious Revolution in the seventeenth century, and in America a century later, in 1776. It could be the power and ideological vacuum after the death of an overwhelming, overpowering leader, as it was in China in the mid-1970s.

In India's case, the crisis was less dramatic (although it certainly didn't seem so at the time) and was caused by economic and emotional meltdown. It was the spring of 1991, the harbinger of a tempestuous year for India's politics and its economy. There was fear of humiliation, a chance that India might default on its repayments to the World Bank. It was a matter of honor for every Indian.

The fact that India was mired in an unprecedented balance of payments mess by 1990 is well known. But for me, what remains etched in memory is some disquieting news I heard in July 1991. A British Airways flight had left Mumbai for London with a consignment of 4.78 metric tons (4.89 tons) of gold from the vaults of the Reserve Bank of India to be retained by the Bank of England as collateral for future borrowings.

Before the ink had dried on this news, reports appeared that another consignment of 19.91 metric tons (21.95 tons) of gold had been sent to London. This was followed by a third and a fourth consignment over the next 10 days. In all, 46.91 metric tons (51.71 tons) of gold were flown out. These four consignments, it was said, were just enough to raise $400 million (Rs 15.92 billion).

This transfer of gold was in line with the report that had come a few days before my party, the Congress, assumed office, stating that the previous government had got India's largest bank—the State Bank of India, fully owned by the government until then—to swap 20 metric tons (22.05 tons) of gold to raise a repayable loan of $240 million (about Rs 9.55 billion). The money was urgently needed to meet sovereign payment schedules.

The then-governor of the RBI, S. Venkitaramanan, did his best to assuage public sentiment, dismay and anger. By law, he pointed out, the RBI was required to keep a minimum of 85 percent of its gold reserves within the country. "India has adequate gold reserves," he emphasized. But somehow such logic was not enough.

The Indian relationship with gold is unique. For generations and centuries, gold has been a sort of social security blanket, the last recourse in times of war, famine, or political turmoil. Of course, this situation is changing now, with new instruments of investment (mutual funds and equities) becoming familiar to even ordinary middle-class folk, but, according to the World Gold Council and GFMS *Gold Survey*, India still remains the world's leading consumer and net importer of gold, accounting for a fifth of global consumption. In 2006 alone, India's figures for consumption and import of gold were higher than those of the United States, China, and Turkey—all big gold consumers—put together.

There is a deep emotional relationship between Indians and gold that cannot be understood using the tools of economists and econometricians; it has long survived the world's coming off the gold standard. In 1962, when India was invaded by the Chinese army, ordinary Indians responded by donating to a special defense fund. Many families, including mine, gave their gold and jewelry to the fund. That is why sending India's gold out of the country was a blow to collective self-esteem.

Moreover, this was not a well-timed transaction aimed at getting a good price; it was a distress sale. As Venkitaramanan was to write years later:

> We argued in vain that we should be allowed to pledge the gold while keeping it in our territory, since the RBI was already an international depository for the IMF's [International Monetary Fund's] gold. But this argument did not prevail. The international lenders insisted on our moving the gold physically out of India's borders.

This insistence itself was an indication of how low India's credibility had fallen.

The most visible aspect of the financial crisis of 1991 was the balance of payments (BOP) problem. India was not much of a trading nation then; its trade-to-GDP ratio was not even one-third of what it is today. Its import order books were marked by two "F" words: fuel and fertilizer. Besides, Rajiv Gandhi, during his tenure as prime minister between 1984 and 1989, had given impetus to the modernization of industry, and as a result India had developed an additional appetite for capital goods. After years of being denied access to new technology imports and with signs of increased demand, industry went ahead and set up new capacities through imports. This ran up huge BOP deficits, but it was a calculated gamble that required sustained support and a subsequent plan for liberalization.

This plan was partially derailed by the defeat of the Indian National Congress—my party—in the 1989 election. Between 1989 and 1991, fractious coalition governments ran India. As the 1991 election approached, Rajiv had a blueprint for economic reform ready. It had actually been drawn up in 1989 and would have been implemented if the party had won that year's election. As it happened, history was cruel to Rajiv. He was assassinated by a terrorist group midway through the 1991 election campaign. A month later, in June 1991, the Congress Party came to power, bereft of its inspirational leader, but with his road map in hand.

Meanwhile, government finances had spun out of control. There was suddenly an absolute lack of liquidity. The turmoil in West Asia arising out of Saddam Hussein's invasion of Kuwait and the first Gulf War had sent oil prices soaring. In 1991, as a third government fell in 17 months, India's internal politics looked inscrutable enough to provoke rating agencies into downgrading the country's ratings. Indian workers and professionals living abroad (nonresident Indians, or NRIs, as they are called) generally arbitraged high interest rates paid on term deposits by Indian banks. Now they began to withdraw money, wary of future risks.

But the real problem was the short-term debt that India had

contracted through "bankers' acceptances," a financial instrument that does not easily lend itself to rollovers and is therefore poison for countries devoid of comfortable foreign exchange reserves. When the call came to honor the bankers' acceptances, there was nothing left in the RBI's coffers. The IMF was willing to bail out India, but it wanted the country to pledge its gold as an act of good faith.

Apart from the symbolism of the gold transfer, other economic indexes also looked grim. GDP growth had tapered off to 1.4 percent in 1991–1992. Food grain and industrial production growth rates had turned negative. Added to this was the agony of high inflation, the wholesale price index having risen 16 percent in August 1991. Manmohan Singh, a respected economist, had just taken over as finance minister in the Congress cabinet of Prime Minister P. V. Narasimha Rao. He gave a chilling account of the economic crisis in his first budget speech on July 24, 1991:

> There is no time to lose. Neither the Government nor the country can live beyond its means year after year. The room for manoeuvre, to live on borrowed money or time, does not exist any more. Any further postponement of macro-economic adjustment, long overdue, would mean that the balance of payments situation, now exceedingly difficult, would become unmanageable and inflation, already high, would exceed limits of tolerance . . . there can be no adjustment without pain. The people must be prepared to make necessary sacrifices to preserve our economic independence and restore the health of our economy.

Rereading this speech after so many years, it sounds like one made during wartime, but it was actually the opening gambit for long-term reform. History was to validate Manmohan Singh and his chosen path. Between June 1991, when he was sworn in as finance minister in the Rao cabinet, and May 2004, when he took the oath as prime minister of the Congress-led United Progressive Alliance (UPA) government, five prime ministers had driven in and out of South Block, the British-built offices perched atop Raisina Hill, the manicured hillock in central Delhi that serves as the political nerve center of India. These were men with various ideological leanings, ranging from a leader of southern India's farming communities, to a Soviet-era socialist intellectual, to the most recognizable figure in India's socially conservative religious right. But what was remarkable about Manmohan Singh's economic action of 1991 was that it wasn't seriously challenged by any of the subsequent governments. In a sense, he firewalled it from politics. If you are looking for a Western comparison, it lies perhaps in post-1979 Britain, where Margaret Thatcher's road map became conventional wisdom, for the Conservatives, of course, but even for the Tony Blair–Gordon Brown New Labour.

India's modern age began in 1991, although this is likely to be contested by many people who are not inclined to accept that India has moved forward vigorously enough. This is partially true, at best. India is, after all, at once modern, postmodern, medieval, ancient, perennial, ever-changing, and unchanging. There is perhaps no major economy in the world (and India is among the four largest) that lives in such an intersection of time warps. In no other democracy do everyday economic issues, like whether pension funds should be allowed to invest members' savings partly in the stock market, coexist with matters that are outright spiritual: should it be the duty of the government to facilitate the building of a shrine? India, in that sense, is at a crossroads. But it is not possible to ignore the distance the country has covered, all of it through a conscious political choice. Changing course from the past was not an easy task—or even entirely desirable. The reform of 1991 was a milestone; the journey continues.

Against All Odds

Before he became finance minister, Manmohan Singh had been chief economic advisor to the government. As such, he had his finger on the fading pulse of the economy. At one of the earliest meetings of the cabinet (as finance minister), he made a presentation on the state of the economy and the steps he had decided to take. His agenda, it was soon apparent, would sound the death knell for licensing and myriad other systems of state control of business investments and expansion. It would, therefore, throw existing businesses into the choppy waters of competition. Besides, the decision to reduce the many subsidies, even if they were only capped and not actually rolled back, would pose a threat to the populism that traditional politicians and businesses had become addicted to.

The clearest break from the past in Manmohan Singh's 1991 reform lay in his Statement of Industrial Policy. One sentence still rings in my ears; it was revolutionary: "Industrial licensing will henceforth be abolished for all industries, except those specified, irrespective of levels of investment." The exception was now the rule.

As industrial licensing went out the window, so did the complex import licensing system. To buy a machine from abroad, for example, one no longer had to "persuade" an influential official in the government to get permission. Those who needed imports in order to export (like a diamond jeweler) were issued import entitlements (called Eximscrips), which they could trade at a market-determined exchange rate. This was among the first steps toward freeing the rupee.

This development, coupled with a 21 percent devaluation of the rupee, created the platform for aggressive export growth, for the first time, perhaps, in modern India. In 1990–1991, exports were a meager 7.2 percent of GDP; today (2006–2007) they are in excess of 23 percent. A friend of mine, who managed a hospital, came to my house one day in 1991 with a bouquet of flowers. He wanted to congratulate the government, he said, for enabling him to import his first body scan machine.

There was a ripple effect across middle-income India. Imported intermediate inputs brought down the prices of locally made refrigerators, washing machines, and kitchen appliances, not to mention television sets and automobiles. Significantly, in early 1992, India shifted to a dual exchange rate regime in which exporters were allowed to sell 60 percent of their foreign exchange in the free market and obligated to sell only 40 percent to the government at a lower "official" rate. Exchange rate unification followed, and the market exchange rate became the single rate. From 1994 on, the government having accepted current account convertibility, Indians could freely buy foreign exchange for study or treatment abroad or just for foreign travel. The dollar ceased to be a symbol of contraband.

This, of course, posed a major threat to the protected citadels of family-owned traditional industry, which went under the generic label of the "Bombay Club." But the welcome accorded to Manmohan Singh's reformist budget had been so widespread that nobody was really unambiguously opposed. No one was running the policy down, even though there was an obvious element of panic at the sudden change. Stalwarts of the Bombay Club-2 met the finance minister on August 11, pleading, among other things, that the "threat" of foreign takeover of their businesses now appeared to be real following the permission for 51 percent foreign equity participation in a variety of industries.

A ringing rebuff to the cringing by the Bombay Club members came from a colossus of the 1940s Bombay Club, J. R. D. Tata, who was still alive. In a signed article in the *Times of India* ("Berlin

Walls Should Fall"), Tata wrote: "I am saddened, though not surprised, to find that several critics of the NIP [New Industrial Policy] have denounced this as anti-Nehruvian, which only shows how little they knew of the dynamic mind of Pandit Nehru which, faced with the havoc created in the economy, would have been the first among the first to salute the NIP." The 88-year-old doyen of industrial enterprise, whose group had set up India's first modern hotel, first steel plant, and first airline, was clearly overwhelmed by emotion. He ended the article on a high patriotic pitch: "Let the world now say, 'A new tiger has emerged in Asia—a tiger uncaged.'" And that was in 1991, soon after the reforms had been announced. Today, India has already embarked on a path that would have gratified that stalwart of Indian industry.

Tightrope Walk

In the heady aftermath of the 1991 reform, a tendency to paint the 1980s as a decade of missed opportunities arose. This is unfair criticism. This decade not only provided but also facilitated the buildup to the 1990s. Big changes were foreseen; it was accepted that the *ancien régime* couldn't sustain quick economic growth. But there was no magic moment, no breaching of the Bastille, no equivalent, despite J. R. D. Tata's comparison, of the demolition of the Berlin Wall. Instead, tariff rates were raised substantially in the 1980s, helping domestic producers to earn their "rent" and the government to rake in tariff revenues.

In 1998, the World Trade Organization (WTO) calculated that in 1990–1991, the highest tariff rate in India had stood at 355 percent, the average of all tariff rates at 113 percent, and the import-weighted average of tariff rates at 87 percent. Prudently, Manmohan Singh rolled back tariffs in stages (we are still doing so). He brought the top rate down to 50 percent by 1995–1996, his final year as finance minister. But the beauty of Manmohan Singh's tariff reform was that he set it on a long-run movement toward liberalization without abandoning domestic industry to reel under an import shock.

Though the Congress Party lost the 1996 general election and remained out of power through the rest of the 1990s, the reform process it had set off proved irreversible. Indeed, it initiated much that was achieved later. It began the process of opening up telecommunications, with the advent of the first private mobile phone companies. By the end of the 1990s, reform in telecommunications had pitted the state monopoly against fierce competition from private players, not only giving a decisive edge to the growth of nontraditional communication technologies (cellular, Internet, Voice Over Internet Protocol) but paving the way for India's emergence as the ultimate destination for offshoring.

The Congress government of 1991–1996 also made key institutional changes that, in later years, served India well and earned it admiration among the emerging economies. The transformation of the financial sector and changes in its governance were dramatic. An office called Controller of Capital Issues, in a rather Kafkaesque manner, was summarily abolished.

When ingenious stock market swindlers subverted the stock market in 1992–1993, the liberalization process suffered a small setback. Very soon, the government, which had already put a regulator in place, made sure the regulator was given substantial powers. It worked. Today, the Securities and Exchange Board of India (SEBI) stands strong with unflinching credibility. This increased investor confidence as the stock market became more transparent. India gradually witnessed a change, with public subscription to shares becoming a principal source of equity capital within a few years. This allowed entrepreneurs to grow without full dependence on the age-old banks and their discretionary systems for allocation of funds. Foreign capital also learned to trust the Indian markets that much more. In 2005–2006, close to 900 foreign institutional investors invested about $9.5 billion in the Indian bourses. The cumulative stock of FII investment in India has exceeded $60 billion. This would not have been possible if a streamlining of the stock market system had not begun and the law giving teeth to SEBI had not been set up in the early years of the reform process.

Legacy of a Summer

When he was asked to assess the impact of the French Revolution, the Chinese Communist leader Chou En-Lai is reported to have said, "It is too early to tell." How did the heady, tempestuous, and eventually epoch-making summer of 1991 change India? Frankly, it is tempting to invoke Chou's sentiments. The changes have been so sweeping—are so overwhelming—that they have, sometimes literally, transformed the way Indians live and work, eat and entertain themselves. One economist evocatively described it as the "summer of economic independence," to complement "Freedom at Midnight." Its legacy surrounds citizens of India today: in India's galloping GDP numbers, in its rising trade figures, in its IT and telecommunication boom stories, in the transformation of high-tech manufacture, in the very reason this book is being written—and read.

The principal legacies of 1991 can be divided into two "i" categories: individual and institutional. The reforms of the summer of 1991—or, more accurately, the policy changes of 1991–1993—triggered a shift in mindset. Social and entrepreneurial energies that had been bottled up were suddenly released, with a force and a magnificence that astounded even Indians. One generation of Indians was enabled to dream dreams that would have been unimaginable to these people's parents.

With the end of the licensing raj, as a slew of regulations were dismantled, technocrats and engineers, professional managers and accountants, software programmers, and even civil servants gave up secure jobs to chase their visions, set up companies—and become entrepreneurs. This heralded the age of individualism and triggered, in the early 1990s, the first of two recent real estate booms. True, property prices rose and fell and rose again—a cycle that takes place everywhere—but the process led to a vast reduction in the average age of first-time home buyers.

As incomes and expectations rose, as consumer credit began to be disbursed more easily, the members of a generation that had seen its fathers and mothers move into their own homes only in their late fifties began picking up property in their thirties. Life in the old India had been a struggle for necessities; for a middle-class person, the pinnacle of achievement was getting an out-of-turn allotment of an LPG cooking cylinder from a parliamentarian's discretionary quota, bypassing a long waiting list and ending an arduous struggle for a rudimentary necessity. Liberation from this low-expectation regimen was cathartic.

The second achievement of the Congress government of 1991–1996 was putting in place the institutional framework that laid the basis for fueling the current rapid economic growth, the so-called Indian economic miracle. There were key policy changes in 1991 and 1992. In 1993 and 1994, India was convulsed by the debate over the WTO, which was then being negotiated under relentless scrutiny and with nearly unprecedented acrimony by more than 100 countries. In India, the government was criticized for allegedly "giving away too much" at the WTO and for even discussing the Dunkel Draft (which defined the eventual WTO agreement) at all. Scare stories abounded: the East India Company would be back; the WTO would wipe out Indian manufacturing and services; the country would become a colony again. For the government and its negotiators, it was a leap of faith. Looking back at those days, it becomes obvious that many owe the Congress apologies for the misplaced fervor with which its government was attacked over the WTO agreement.

It was not just big-picture institutions that were set up or joined. As environment minister, for instance, I decided to strengthen the industrial pollution regulatory system. It was clear after the Earth Summit of 1992 that the toxic impact of industrial growth and the looming specter of climate change were potential pitfalls for an emerging India. The Central Pollution Control Board already existed, but it was overhauled. Daughter pollution control boards were set up in all states, and their technical capacities were enhanced. A system was put in place that ensured that no industrial unit could be set up without a comprehensive environmental impact audit. When this system was being discussed in the early 1990s, many people thought that it was a waste of time. By the end of the decade, they were congratulating me for taking early steps.

Finally, the biggest achievement of the Congress government was that it took the plunge at all, that it actually changed India's economic course. In May 2004, in the midst of national elections in India, the former prime minister, P. V. Narasimha Rao, was asked by a interviewer what he thought of the then BJP government's taking exclusive credit for economic reforms. The BJP's election pitch had surprised and amused some of us from the original reformist government of 1991. It was as if there had been no economic liberalization, no economy even, before the BJP came to power. Rao gave a typically clever, typically inscrutable answer: "Taking something from 50 to 100 is making it double. But if you take it from 0 to 1, how many times is it?" The interviewer answered the question: "It's infinite." Rao went on, "Infinite; and what it really entails is a complete U-turn without seeming to be a U-turn. . . . So the question for you to consider is: which is more difficult?"

The answer has always been obvious—at least for those who were fortunate enough to be in that "war room" in the summer of 1991 as India fought off its most threatening economic crisis.

Chapter 4

The Gap Years

In politics, it is important to not only do the right thing but to be *seen* to do the right thing. This is not to build a case for deception; it is just that the "optics" is vital. A similar type of situation is faced by a business organization that is seeking an image overhauling and turning itself around—or for a country presenting itself as a potential economic powerhouse and competing with the rest of the emerging markets as an attractive investment destination. Chrysler's admirable restructuring in the 1980s would not have been recognized as a signal achievement had it not been driven by the flamboyance of Lee Iacocca's personality. Yet, even the best, most committed and articulate "salespersons" for economic reform sometimes cannot achieve it all. China's prodigious GDP growth, for instance, has never quite effaced the nagging doubt—always there, even if rarely expressed—that the notion of "market socialism," and of a free-market economy coexisting with a dominant one-party communist polity, represents a circle that will, one day, have to be squared.

Through the 1990s and well into the first decade of the new century, a similar predicament beset India, or rather perceptions of India. Simply put, its internal politics and tumult at times seemed to send out mixed signals about where the country was headed and what sort of future India saw for itself. There were many rocky missteps in India's early journey toward a present-day economy. In December 1992, a year and a half after Manmohan Singh's history-making budget speech that heralded economic reform, India saw its biggest religious conflagration in a long time. A shrine in Ayodhya where, allegedly, a Hindu temple had been destroyed in the sixteenth century to build a Muslim mosque (Babri Masjid), was torn down by Hindu extremists. This act of infamy led to religious violence across India, including weeks of bloodletting in India's business capital, Mumbai (Bombay).

A banker friend of mine from London, visiting India in early 1993, told me that the demolition of the Babri Masjid and the subsequent storm had done for the perception of India what the Tiananmen Square incident did for China in 1989. I told him a few years later that his observation was hasty, as global investment in China began to rise steadily after the Tiananmen Square incident. Investors were probably reassured that there wasn't any serious challenge to the Chinese political leadership. When I visited the McDonald's outlet on Tiananmen Square, said to be the world's largest McDonald's restaurant, which opened a decade after the mayhem, I could not help noticing the vast difference between the West's professed love for democracy and the cold calculations that guide business investments.

When they enter a new country, investors and business corporations are betting on the stability of both politics and the polity. In the mid-1990s, India didn't offer much reassurance to those who had just gotten to know it. When the Congress government was voted out of power in 1996, it was replaced by three governments in two years. The first lasted just 13 days and didn't win a majority vote in Parliament; in the second and third, an assortment of regional and state-level parties combined to form the United Front. By the winter of 1997, the second United Front government had also fallen, and fresh elections were called. This became a feature for India in that roller-coaster decade.

Parliamentary elections in India are scheduled every five years. In the period between 1990 and 1999, they were due to be held twice; instead, my country saw four such elections—in 1991, 1996, 1998, and 1999. In only one of those years was a government reelected. Compared to the unchanging, unaltering nature of governments in certain other countries—the entire Asian swathe from Singapore to China, or from predemocracy South Korea to Suharto-era Indonesia—India may have seemed like a risky gamble. Would democracy prove too much of an inhibition on India's economic potential? An article in the journal *Foreign Affairs* said:

> Conventional wisdom aside, the main threat India faces is economic. Slower growth and a stalled program of economic reforms could endanger India's stability. Its politics, by contrast, exhibit an admirable ability to bring extremists, including the Hindu nationalists of the newly preeminent Bharatiya Janata Party, closer to the center.

India's democracy is the glue that keeps the country together; its economy, if not reformed, could cause dangerous strains,

Some businessmen voted with their feet. In the mid-1990s, unsure of whether India would stay the course, the pharmaceutical giant Merck decided to leave. At a World Economic Forum meeting in Davos, Switzerland, in 2005, the company's CEO confessed to me that, in retrospect, this had been a big mistake. Ironically, at the same conference, the CEO of Pfizer told me that his company (one of Merck's major rivals among the big pharmaceuticals) had thought of leaving India in the 1990s but had been persuaded to stay on "by the man who is now prime minister—Dr. Manmohan Singh." I thought of asking him how many thousands of dollars in consultants' fees the well-meaning Manmohan Singh had saved Pfizer with his sage and eventually correct counsel; instead, I bit my lip, smiled politely, and moved on. Come to think of it, we were doing a lot of that in India in the mid-1990s—biting our lips, smiling politely, and moving on.

As it happened, not everyone shared this innate Indian equanimity. Instead, people were puzzled by what they thought were mixed and paradoxical signs from India. In 1998, within weeks of coming to office, the BJP-led government exploded a nuclear device, carrying out India's first nuclear tests in almost 25 years. There were no real disagreements between India's mainstream political parties concerning the country's right to possess nuclear technology. It was the Congress governments of Nehru and Indira Gandhi that had encouraged Indian scientists to pursue nuclear technology for civilian ends, to fulfill energy needs. In 1974, Indira Gandhi had also given the go-ahead for India's first nuclear test. Yet, even while China became a nuclear weapons state and Pakistan clandestinely pursued the Bomb, India refused to develop weapons. It also refused to sign the Nuclear Non-Proliferation Treaty because of its discriminatory nature.

There was a sharp reaction to the Indian nuclear tests of 1998. The United States imposed economic sanctions, Japan cut off developmental funding, the World Bank deferred a $865 million loan package, and Australia downgraded defense ties—and these are only random examples. To me this event was an eye-opener in the sense that is the central message of the iconic film *Rashomon* by Japanese filmmaker Akira Kurosawa, external and internal perceptions of the same phenomenon were very different.

In June 1998, a month after the nuclear tests, a businessman friend visited me from Canada. We had a vigorous, lively, and sometimes edgy exchange.

"I can't understand your country," he started. "Why do you want the Bomb?"

"I don't necessarily want the Bomb," I said. "We are the country of Mahatma Gandhi; we certainly don't want to *use* the Bomb. But we live in a tough neighborhood, and we're not going to have somebody else tell us that we cannot legitimately pursue the nuclear option. Yet, India's real strength is its soft power, its cultural products and influence. This is the weaponry of the future. Nuclear bombs are yesterday's toys."

The twentieth century saw more bloodshed and more lives lost in warfare than any previous century in recorded history. It was the century of hard power. In contrast, despite the terrorism and the violence it has begun with, I am confident that the twenty-first century will be the century of soft power. A nation's cultural and human resources, its intellectual and entrepreneurial energies, are going to define its global status.

As the twenty-first century approached, it was already a cliché that Britain's new national dish was chicken tikka masala. Indian music and cinema were popular and had name recognition in regions as far apart as Central Asia and North Africa. Yoga was already a lifestyle enhancer for the trendy set on America's coasts. The caliber of Indian Institute of Technology (IIT) graduates was beginning to stir up Silicon Valley. Indian software writers were taking charge of the battle against Y2K and would soon render it the biggest non-event in history. Rajnikanth, a Tamil-language movie star whose gravity-defying stunts made him an icon in India's south, also commanded a huge market in, funnily enough, Japan. Ironically, his movies were not always dubbed into Japanese.

So what did India see itself as? What vision did we have of our country in the twenty-first century? Was it one of an outward-looking soft power that was confident of its economic wherewithal, its scholarship and cerebration, and the breadth of its cultural product line? Alternatively, was it one of a hard power, obsessed with nuclear weapons and medieval religious disputes, prone to regular occurrences of religiopolitical violence? Was India, to adapt Churchill's famous description of Russia, "a paradox wrapped in a contradiction inside a conundrum"? To an outsider, these were fair questions in the summer of 1998.

New Ideas, Old Contests

Between 1996, when a Congress prime minister left office, and 2004, when the next Congress prime minister entered office, India saw much political oscillation. In this period, it had five governments and three prime ministers (one of them becoming prime minister three times, to add to the statistical confusion). In a sense, an entire nation, a whole society, was trying to make up its mind about where it was headed and what direction it wanted to take. It was a churning process. Essentially, India was caught between left-over baggage from the political battles of the 1980s and the future that beckoned in the new millennium. Some old shibboleths needed to be laid to rest, and some pernicious ideas had to reach closure before India could move ahead.

In terms of economic policy making, India's apparent fitfulness was rooted in a series of governments made up of political parties that were opposed to the Congress Party coming to power. Each of these governments was convinced that it knew the magic formula to fine-tune, to "fix" and calibrate the process of liberalization that Manmohan Singh had begun. In this attempt, the entire gamut of the Indian political system came to control the government at one time or another: State and regional or caste-based parties provided prime ministers and defense ministers. The Communist Party of India entered the national government and ran the Home (Interior) Ministry. Finally, the right-wing Bhartiya Janta Party (BJP) ruled India from 1998 to 2004.

The BJP-led government was quick to implement "first generation reforms," that is, reforms that do not attract strong political resistance. Heading up a coalition of 24 parties, as is customary in India's fragmented polity, it was careful not to ruffle too many feathers by being too daring on reforms. But it set up effective institutions to set further reforms in motion—like creating the Telecom Regulatory Authority of India for the telecommunication sector and giving power to an electricity regulator by enacting comprehensive legislation in 2003. And it carried forward a slew of projects of far-reaching importance, like the Golden Quadrilateral highway development project. On economic issues, there was hardly a visible gap in reform policy in the 1990s.

It was a tribute to the Congress Party that despite their initial rhetoric, not one of these governments moved away from the path that Manmohan Singh had walked down as finance minister. Instead, income tax rates continued to come down. And, as the new century began, privatization began to take place, and the groundwork was laid for the telecom revolution. To the world, this seemed a sort of validation that economic reform had come to stay.

So, were the 1990s a showcase for the Great Indian Paradox, the coexistence of forward-looking economics and stagnant or at times regressive politics? Although this may have seemed to be true for a while, to my mind there was a more serious paradox at play, a genuine contest between new and old mindsets that external observers never entirely understood or empathized with.

My party's government, led by Rajiv Gandhi (prime minister from 1984 to 1989), was perceptibly cleaved by the "digital divide." Many of those born before, say, 1940 had the firm opinion that computers were no more than a secretarial aid. Unlike today's generation, which is computer dependent, the earlier generation was caught between thinking of the computer as a new gizmo and as an instrument that could challenge the established hierarchy. In the 1990s, India was right in the middle of the Schumpeterian "creative destruction." A trade unionist friend who spent many years fighting computerization in banks argues, "A single ATM would put 20 clerks out of a job." I did not doubt his estimate of an automated teller machine's ability to render clerical jobs redundant, but I also could see that it was not possible to stop a technological revolution that was making business more efficient, besides creating many more jobs elsewhere and making things easier for customers.

This was also a period of debate on the exact role of the state in the economy and its management. The old offices of "controllers" and super-regulators still existed, but they had less and less to do. The idea that life in India, particularly economic life, had perhaps been too tied to the government's apron strings had begun to crystallize. The old mindset was being challenged, but, while rules could be liberalized, it took time to change attitudes. In the years since independence, successive generations of civil servants had come to see themselves as custodians of the greater common good, "protecting" society from the private sector, and they were institutionally suspicious of free enterprise. But the old order was yielding ground.

In the process, the old-fashioned civil servants suddenly became very lonely. In 1992, as environment minister, I traveled to the National Academy of Administration in Mussoorie, where senior civil servants are trained. The director proudly introduced me to the members of his faculty, telling me that they were very experienced. "That must be your liability," I retorted. The director was aghast, but was nice enough to appreciate the joke. Today, of course, the shift from economic arbiter/actor to regulator/facilitator is far more pronounced among civil servants. Governance is becoming a synthesis of politicians, generalist bureaucrats, and technocrats, with specialists playing a substantial policy-making role in sectors as far apart as the environment and power. But it took a full decade and the retirement of a generation for this to take effect.

Second, the expectations revolution among citizens made democracy seem a far harder taskmaster than ever before. When the Asian tigers were revamping their economies, they had the luxury of time. If the government made an unpopular decision, it could wait out the immediate resentment. These countries absorbed the short-term pain to achieve long-term gain; their political systems allowed it. But in India, an election (a major state election if not a national one) is almost always at the most two years away, and a price must be paid for unpopular decisions. Therefore, the gestation period for public policy change in India often has to be no more than 24 to 30 months; if it is longer, politicians tend to balk. I will draw an analogy here: The U.S. House of Representatives elects its members every two years. Imagine what would happen if all economic decision making for the country, and by the administration, had to follow this punishing schedule. Yet this is India's reality. In the 1990s, it seemed to be the political scientist's nightmare.

Meanwhile, in Rural India . . .

Economic change is not always a front-loaded process. The first signs of change in the economy were felt in urban consumer and job markets. Rural India, where you could sometime travel hundreds of miles without seeing a factory, felt out of the loop. Even when people's skill sets were similar, there appeared to be a lack of equal opportunity. A young man from Chhindwara, my predominantly rural parliamentary constituency, came to me a few years ago. At great financial sacrifice, his parents had managed to educate him, and he had a master's degree in computer applications, an MCA. In a booming IT market, he should have been snapped up, just as his fellow MCAs from cities and towns were. But here he was, without a job, asking me to help. There was both a pent-up energy and a pent-up resentment. It was all a matter of which would come first—the job or the next election. There was no point telling this boy that the economy was growing at 8 or 9 percent and that software exports were galloping along. He would have shrugged his shoulders and said, "In that case, why am I still unemployed?"

With some small help from me, the boy with the MCA eventually found a job with a big IT firm in Hyderabad. And, as I tried to understand his problem, I drew a lesson from it. I realized that, although this boy was equipped with an appropriate degree, he had a cultural disconnect from an industry that thrived in an urban setting. And the spectrum of such industries was expanding fast. New opportunities were and are opening up in retail, banking, pharmaceuticals, and hospitality, not to mention IT and ITES (IT-enabled services). It is not that there is a real talent crunch for the new businesses. Instead, it is the rural-urban disconnect that is creating an artificial shortage as it hobbles the small-town boy's personality and self-confidence.

The youth in India today are divided between two groups. One of them responds to the world through some sort of a screen—a desktop, a laptop, or even a mobile phone. The other group doesn't yet have such a screen as its intermediary with the world. There is a cultural divide, and an economic divide too. This realization prompted me to persuade NIIT (an Indian company that is a leader in computer education) to set up a knowledge center for IT professionals at Chhindwara. This center also runs a finishing school and offers intensive, short-duration computer courses for graduates in the district. I have no doubt that the small-town graduate is in no way inferior to his urban peers, except for lacking a Western orientation in his interpersonal relationships.

If this little experiment with the knowledge center that has begun in my district succeeds, it may pave the way for the most inclusive graduate job program in the country. By supporting this program, NIIT will also have shielded to some extent the IT industry which now faces a backlash because of its disconnect with the "real India." The crux of the rural unemployment problem lies with the semiliterate and illiterate population that is still engaged in agriculture. If the 1996–2004 period is put under the scanner, the real paradox in India is to be found in two sets of figures. Agriculture today accounts for only 18.5 percent of GDP (in 2006–2007), but it employs about 60 percent of the workforce. In developed countries, agriculture employs no more than 5 percent of the labor force. China's case is startling. In just about 50 years, it shifted almost half the work force engaged in agriculture to industry.

In contrast, only 18 percent of the Indian workforce is in industry and 23 percent in services. This is the real Indian paradox. Addressing this discrepancy is the challenge for any government. In the 1990s, in the first burst of economic opening up, most of the jobs being created were in services, and the workforce was stuck in agriculture. The revival of Indian manufacturing was still a few years away; the extra hands on the farm had nowhere to go. Given their limited education, they couldn't automatically become ITES professionals and staff the business process outsourcing units in

Bangalore. This was a crucial transition phase during which people were genuinely concerned about their future.

Things got worse for rural India when agricultural growth began to slacken in the 1990s. In that decade, for the first time since the Green Revolution of the 1960s, the rate of growth of the population outpaced the rate of growth of food grain production. In 1990–1992 agricultural GDP grew at an average of about 1 percent a year, and between 1995–1996 and 2002–2003, agricultural GDP grew at an average of just 1.7 percent a year. Public spending on agriculture, which is crucial in areas such as irrigation, began to decline as governments became more fiscally conscious. Obviously, there was anguish and frustration for the farmer, who was buffeted by larger economic forces over which he had no control.

For irrigation needs, for the purchase of fertilizers and seeds, and even for personal family reasons, farmers were slowly but surely being sucked into a debt trap. In 1991, the National Sample Survey (NSS) reported, Indian cultivators collectively owed Rs 144.62 billion ($3.63 billion). By 2002, the NSS said that this had ballooned to Rs 667.53 billion ($16.78 billion). Farmer suicides were becoming a frequent, and shaming, story in the news media, particularly in the cotton-growing regions of Maharashtra and Andhra Pradesh, two of India's largest and most industrialized states.

The contrast was simply too strong. One India was riding a housing and automobile boom on the back of cheap consumer credit. Another India was being forced into suicide because it couldn't pay back its loans. It was not rich commercial farmers who were suffering. Rather, it was subsistence farmers who were unable to repay what were, really, small sums of money, no more than a few thousand rupees in many cases, because the rains had failed or the crops had been destroyed by a natural calamity. Some farmers take loans from government or cooperative banks. Many, however, are still trapped in debt by village loan sharks who have established themselves in the local community over decades, lending money at usurious rates of interest that could reach even to 150 percent a year.

It is a poignant story. A farmer, modest but proud, working in his field deep in the interior of India was so hurt, his self-esteem so shaken by his inability to service his debt, that he felt death was the only recourse. It said something about the Indian farmer and the Indian ethos: a man's word was his honor. Faced with similar circumstances in 1991, the Indian government mortgaged its gold; for hundreds of farmers, there was no collateral to sell off.

A New Beginning

As I began my current term as minister in 2004, it was difficult not to appreciate the changes that India had undergone since my previous term in government (1991–1996). First, the ball that the Congress had set rolling in that somber, trepidation-filled summer of 1991 had acquired a momentum of its own. There was a sense of hope, purpose, and derring-do. In contrast to, say, the 1970s, social attitudes had altered. A distributional society had given way to an aspirational society. Across the nation, in both rural and urban areas, the climbers were aspiring and aspirers were consuming. The horizon of expectations was expanding at all levels. The prevailing conviction was no longer that "life should be better for my children." Instead, it was that "life should get better for me," and in the next few years, if not right now.

Second, Indian democracy had demonstrated its capacity to reconcile differences and incorporate dissent without changing the nature of the political system. It could steer the boat of economic change away from the choppy waters of populist protest. This made India appear superficially hot and turbulent, but it was calm and stable at the base—quite in contrast to China, as others have pointed out. As a Japanese business executive once put it, "It is easy to enter China but difficult to stay there. It is difficult to enter India but relatively easier to stay on."

Policy change in India is a grueling mixer-blender type of process, but once it happens, it is usually adhered to. In terms of compliance with international treaties, it must be realized that India has one of the best records in the world. This may be a country that takes a long time to agree to what the rules should be, but once it does agree, it plays by them. Over the past decade, almost every major national and regional party has been part of one government or another. They have had their views and differences, their own opinions on the pace and acceleration of change. Yet the broad thrust of economic policy has not been disturbed. Governments come and go; the process continues.

Chapter 5

Mind over Matter

In the foreign mind, it was Mumbai (Bombay), of all Indian cities, that used to be best suited to evoke a vision of modern India. This was all the more evident when I, as the minister for environment and forests, represented India at the United Nations Conference on Environment and Development—the "Earth Summit," as it was called—in Rio de Janeiro in the summer of 1992. In the course of the conference, which lasted 11 days, I got to know the representatives of a large swath of nation-states, many of them so new that I could barely locate them in a world atlas. Some of them had been born as a result of the breakup of the USSR; others were little specks of land strewn across the Pacific and Indian Oceans. Many of these representatives of new countries, as I could sense, had difficulty in placing New Delhi, the capital, on their mental map of India (unless, of course, they were told that it was close to the Taj Mahal, which brought a glint of recognition to every eye). But Mumbai was known to one and all. The Ukrainian or Moroccan knew it as the home of India's film industry. The man from a little island republic in Micronesia, on the other hand, knew Bombay as a financial center, while the Trinidadian knew the city as the home of Sunil Gavaskar, the cricket legend.

Instead of Mumbai, which had ceased to be the sole iconic city, the new global elite today sees Bangalore (now Bengaluru) when it hears "India." This is particularly true among the New Economy entrepreneurs from the West, who had come up through the venture capital route. Many of them have visited Bengaluru not once but over and over again. And so have western politicians, from Italian Prime Minister Romano Prodi to the British Conservative Party leader David Cameron. In April 2005, Chinese premier Wen Jiabao even began his India visit from Bengaluru, not the national capital.

In the same month, I met Mark Warner, governor of the state of Virginia. "I'm itching to get to Bangalore," he told me. "I want to see where my jobs are going." But my best experience of India's "Bangalorization" was at a famous restaurant in Beijing, where Henry Kissinger had reportedly shown up in public for the first time after two days of secret parleys with Chinese leaders during the 1970s "Ping-Pong diplomacy" phase. A waiter at the restaurant, after helping me carve Peking duck the way it should be carved, gently inquired if I had come from Bangalore, and, if so, how much a course in writing software programs would cost there. I almost dropped my chopsticks in astonishment.

The rise of Bengaluru is a saga of a different IT: India's Transition. However, it does not capture the entire story of India's emergence as the world's ultimate outsourcing destination. The story has just begun and the country is vast, so there may be a hundred Bengalurus waiting to bloom. How India, traditionally a loser in technology races, managed to move to the front of the newest one is certainly a tale worth narrating. However, even this seeming miracle has a prelude.

When the age of steam arrived, India was unlucky in two ways: it wasn't an independent country, and the wealthiest areas of its territory were under the rule of the inventors of the steam engine, the British. Before steam, the territory that was to be known as India had led the world in hand-operated weaving, spinning, and dyeing. In the words of a popular British historian, "The British had first raised tariffs against their [the Indians'] products; then demanded free trade when their [British] alternative industrial mode of production had been perfected." So India missed the first big "power shift" of the past 250 years. This happened not because there were no observant countrymen sitting up to read meaning into the movements of the lid on a simmering kettle, but because the country was a colony.

It is obvious that India's position in the context of IT is not quite comparable with that of Britain in steam power two hundred years ago. Britain left its stamp on everything associated with steam power—the boiler, the cylinder, the piston, the discovery of the laws that govern the expansion and contraction of gas with changes in temperature. In contrast, there is not much of India that you can touch or feel on your computer. I am writing this chapter on a Japanese laptop made in Taiwan, powered by semiconductors made in the United States, using an operating system patented by Microsoft, the U.S. giant. There is certainly an Indian hand behind all these products, but it is invisible to the end-user.

Why? The laptop, the semiconductor, and the operating system are actually products of the IT age, in much the same way that the steam engine that Watt and Boulton made was among the first reliable products of the industrial age. Yet the industrial age is remembered not just for its products, but more for the revolutionary systems it introduced, the most notable among them being the factory system of production. India, for sure, is a much-acclaimed upholder of one of the crucial systems that IT has created: the system of disaggregating production globally (like Adam Smith's division of labor), and then integrating it by using the Internet. In today's parlance, this is known as outsourcing. It is also an accepted fact that outsourcing is at the core of the economic efficiency and competitiveness of businesses.

It is outsourcing that holds the key to global business. Propelled by the power of broad and quick telecommunications networks and the high speed of computation, it is now as integral a part of business as, say, banks or insurance. Outsourcing can be both onshore and offshore. Jobs may be outsourced to sister or daughter firms at home or abroad, or even to third parties in the home country or elsewhere. Whenever a job is parceled out, it essentially involves trade in tasks. And IT, which combines telecommunications with the power of computers, makes this trade in tasks technology-enabled.

Both Texas Instruments's R&D center in India and Toyota's R&D center in Thailand are examples of companies outsourcing strategic tasks to subsidiary firms on foreign soil. India is unbeatable when it comes to obtaining jobs outsourced from abroad to third-party companies. There is no outsourced function in which India lacks the requisite expertise, from simple customer care to managing elaborate sales and marketing data. And India has now moved much further up the value chain, handling jobs that call for domain expertise (knowledge process outsourcing, or KPO), and even handling the entire engineering design cycle activity for a product or service, including the development of the prototype (engineering process outsourcing, or EPO). This has made India's IT skills technology-driven, with their value originating from the multiplicity of their applications.

However, outsourcing is not the only value driver that IT has spawned. There is e-commerce, which hinges on superfast transactions without any middlemen, and thus no cost of intermediation. There is e-governance, the IT-based distribution of public services that guarantees a degree of transparency for citizens and frees them from the tyranny of clerks. In 2006, 22 Indian e-governance projects were declared winners of the Oracle Excellence in e-Governance awards.

IT has unquestionably brought about a drastic transformation in the way we live, with its spin-offs likely to surpass those of the Industrial Revolution. But of all these spin-offs, outsourcing is at once the simplest and the most rewarding. It has ensured a level playing field, and, if given a free rein, it may add untold dimensions to concepts that are accepted as changeless, such as the nation-state, which may acquire a different character as its production processes are increasingly integrated into a global chain of partial jobs. Theoretically, in a perfectly outsourced world, there may still be rich people and poor people, but there should not be differences resulting from some communities enjoying more opportunities for growth and some less, as the Internet is instantaneous and open to all and it leaves little margin for arbitrage in location. It gives the customer a worldwide choice. It makes geography history.

In India's case, the outsourcing/ITES (IT-enabled services) boom was also propelled by the ease with which Indians adapted to the computer, to new machines and technologies. Today, this has put India at the top of the outsourcing pyramid. It holds a 65 percent share of the global market in offshore IT and 45 percent of the worldwide market in ITES.

The difference between the two should not be missed. The former involves the export of software and services for both maintenance and expansion of the target firms' business operations. This may be anything from helping a British bank to measure the risk of a project it is financing in Africa, to helping a supermarket chain in America to reprogram its bills at the checkout counter. At the moment, IT services are growing at 35 percent annually; they hit $18 billion in exports in 2006–2007. On the other hand, ITES involves services that are riding on IT, such as running call centers and writing medical transcriptions or, at a higher level, making cutting-edge designs for a superspecialized drug molecule. Such business process outsourcing (BPO) produced a lower amount, $9 billion, in exports. But it is poised for long-term success. What is the reason?

It is implicit in the architecture of the ITES value chain that India is currently climbing. Leaving the simpler voice-based functions far behind, India has moved up to the highly complex territory of KPO. The journey has been powered by a phenomenal rise in R&D and engineering spending in the Western economies, much of which is being outsourced to knowledge-rich economies like that of India. In a survey of 186 business executives, it was found that

- In 1975, corporations had more than half their R&D sites in their home country.

- By 2004, only a third of the R&D sites were still in home territory.

- While most offshore R&D sites were (in 2004) still in Western Europe or the United States, the number of sites in China and India was growing fast.

In the sheer number of foreign R&D sites, India was ahead of both China and the United States in 2004 and well ahead of Western Europe.

This was possible as a result of the close involvement of Indian firms with high-tech transnational companies (TNCs), particularly in product and process research, which is now turning India into a hub of innovation. Overseeing India's intellectual property (IP) reform is one of the mandates of the Ministry of Commerce and Industry, and it has been a challenge. India is in the midst of an enormous surge in innovation. In 1999–2000, barely seven years ago, there were only 4,824 patent applications in the pipeline. In 2006, the number had shot up six times, to 28,882 applications.

Much of this rising tide of patent applications may be the result of the recent debureaucratization of the process. It is now possible to obtain a patent in eight months; it took eight years in the past. But beneath the surface, it is India's successful engagement with the IT revolution (in contrast to its disengagement from the steam revolution) that is pushing it to the forefront of IP creation. Patent and trademark applications can now be filed electronically. According to the National Association of Software and Services Companies (NASSCOM), the export of engineering services and products is growing at 24 percent annually and contributed $5 billion (Rs 198,950,300) to the kitty last year.

This has made India irresistible to the world's major companies. Cisco Systems, which is a leader in the computer networking business, has publicly announced that it rates India higher than China. Microsoft launched its third research center in India in 2005. Intel has 2,900 engineers working on software and hardware designs for its communication and semiconductor product lines in its center in India. Microsoft Research India is expanding its operations, including the creation of a new research group for cryptography.

And the story certainly doesn't end here. The survey discussed previously shows that after India, which is by far the strongest supply base for IT-ITES services, there are huge stretches of economies "in transition" that have been encouraged by India's success and are now trying to build similar capabilities and gain a slice of the market.

They include China, Russia, South Africa, and a good part of South America. But even as global delivery becomes more distributed, India remains the anchor location, with a 58 percent market share in offshoring of technology IT-BPO.

About three-fourths of the Fortune 500 and at least half the Global 2000 corporations are sourcing technology-related services from India. The nature of global contracts that Indian IT firms win is a testament to the country's journey upward from rudimentary call centers in basements. In 2006, for instance, the big trophies bagged by the Indian IT majors were technology agreements with the world's best-known carmakers, bankers, and airlines.

It is pertinent to ask why, despite India's being an IT power-house, the line "Made in India" does not appear very often in our computer environment. The obvious answer is that in today's world, value tends to get "dematerialized." The "extra something" that India brings to a product is not always capable of being seen, touched, felt, or heard. Yet this added value cannot be ignored. Whether the product is a huge Boeing jet, the relatively small iPhone, or even a Calvin Klein suit, it is the nonmaterial inputs— a patented integrated circuit here or a trendy and aesthetic design there—that make it distinctive. Such nonmaterial value is India's domain.

And it will continue to be so, as knowledge constitutes, and will keep constituting, an ever-increasing share of value. By 2010, global spending on technology, including R&D, is forecast to exceed $2 trillion, of which $110 billion may go offshore. At the current scale of India's success, it is reasonable to expect that the country will grab more than half of this. That squares with the general forecast that India's IT-ITES exports will grow at 20 percent annually until at least 2020.

It also implies an all-round improvement, as the skills that India sells abroad will raise domestic productivity as well. This is putting India high on the organizational map of every large global corporation, including IBM (Big Blue), the crucible of computing. In 2006, this down-to-the-core American company held its annual investors' day on the grounds of the Bangalore Palace. In an even more conspicuous sacrifice of Big Blue's American identity, its retinue of 10,000 employees and quite a few Wall Street investors, not to mention the company's CEO, Sam Palmisano, listened with rapt attention to a speech by the president of India.

On the other hand, the EPO saga comes on the back of India's huge army of engineers, which is growing by about 500,000 every year, and a booming engineering export industry, which has grown nearly seven times, from $833 million (Rs 33.145 billion) in 1985–1986 to $20.3 billion (Rs 807.79 billion) two decades later. This has created a wide dispersal of engineering talents into predominantly small units—1,150, including R&D centers, according to the Engineering Export Promotion Council. Among their clients are leading names in the global automotive, electronics and telecom, and aerospace industries—GM, Ford, Delphi, DaimlerChrysler; Texas Instruments, Sony, Toshiba, Motorola, Dell; Boeing, Pratt & Whitney, Bell Aerospace, Airbus, Rolls-Royce. Of an estimated global EPO market of $140 billion (Rs 5.58 trillion) in 2015, India is likely to draw more than a fifth of the global outsourced demand.

There are many other tasks waiting to be outsourced—legal and educational services and tutoring, or publishing and editing. For outsourcing of knowledge processes, India's competitive advantage lies in its level of comfort with the English language. The anti-outsourcing lobby in the United States and Europe probably thinks it is a waste for lucrative work to be sent to India, almost literally at the click of a mouse. But these people are mistaken. At U.S./European wages, these jobs would have proved unsustainable in the West, hurting profitability, business corporations, shareholders, and ultimately consumers, who would have had to pay more. Outsourcing is a two-way street; it has benefited India, but it has also saved the West a fortune and has helped sustain employment.

Pioneer Program

Though India was on the threshold of independence in 1946, when the first general-purpose electronic computers came into use, it did not wait too long to accept the wonder machines. Nehru's point man in central planning, Mahalanobis, was quick to order a machine from the United States. That was in the 1950s. By then J. R. D. Tata had also ordered a large vacuum tube–based computer, reportedly to keep a check on the tickets of the bus service the Tatas ran in Mumbai. In another 15 years or so, the integrated circuit concept had come, and so had microprocessors; these were milestones in computer architecture, leading to leaps in size, speed, and reliability and to reduced costs.

The defining feature of a computer that distinguishes it from any other machine is that it can be programmed, which means that if a list of instructions (a program) is given to the computer, it will follow those instructions and execute them some time in the future. This led to the birth of a new type of professional: the computer programmer.

As programs got more complex, so did the challenges for the program writers. Indians educated in the post-independence institutions of scientific learning—like the Indian Institutes of Technology (IITs) or the Indian Institute of Science in Bengaluru—proved particularly adept at programming. It is possible that IBM was the first to see their potential. It set up shop in India in the early 1950s. This could really have augured well for India, as it did for Israel and Ireland (both of which are today advanced countries in software development) when TNCs started operations there.

But something happened in India in the 1970s, as a result of which a long winter of protectionism set in. The Foreign Exchange Regulation Act (FERA) of 1973 set a limit on non-Indian stakes in companies. IBM closed its operations, citing concerns about intellectual property. Initially, this seemed to close the gates for IT in India, but the setback was only temporary. For most Indian IT moguls today, the departure of IBM was the trigger for their own entrepreneurship.

At that time, TCS, short for Tata Consultancy Services, was the Indian sales agent for Burroughs, the mainframe manufacturer. TCS began supplying Indian programmers to install system software for a U.S. client of Burroughs. Initially, the exported programmers worked for global firms. Over time, they became professionals specializing in converting the existing application software of end users such as banks into IBM-compatible versions.

By the 1980s, Indian engineers "body shopped" by American corporations had honed their skills in start-ups in the United States and in India. The environment in India began to change when Rajiv Gandhi became prime minister in 1984. He was the first Indian leader to take computers seriously and to understand the vital link between the computer and the telephone. His New Computer Policy (NCP) of 1984, put into effect less than three weeks after he took charge of the government, not only invited foreign firms back but at one stroke also drastically reduced the import tariff on hardware and software. It also recognized software exports as a "delicensed industry," free of the bureaucratic maze of licensing that hamstrung so many other industries, and began a project to set up a chain of software parks (which was implemented in 1991) that would, as Rajiv told me with his characteristic boyish smile, "let the software professional do his work without being bothered by the DoT."

The licensing system and an inefficient telecom monopoly had had a pincer effect on the country's software potential. In his short tenure, Rajiv did his best to bring telecom back to life as well. In his first year in power, he set up two new corporations, in place of a government department with its retinue of civil servants, to provide telecom services in two big cities, Delhi and Mumbai, and subsequently in the rest of the country. It was his policy for opening up the telecom sector that was implemented in 1990 by the government that was then at the helm. However, the 1990s were truly India's "telecom decade": private players came in droves, a regulatory body was put in place, tariffs began sliding down, and, with cellular phones becoming popular, the telephone went from a luxury to a commodity in a flat five years. This brought about a very successful marriage between varied software skills and a reliable telecommunication backbone. The state-induced growth of infrastructure in computers and telecom, at one go, created a platform on which the IT industry could grow naturally.

And if falling telecom costs were a catalyst for change, the big driver for transformation was the Internet and global delivery mechanism, whether in Miami or in Mumbai. From then on, Indian firms began writing programs from home, gradually making body shopping unnecessary. Work started being relocated to India as firms shifted from exporting programs to programming custom software in India. The age of offshore work had begun.

But India's clinching asset was its rising number of science-educated youth, including engineering graduates—the stock of graduate engineers in 2003, for example, was over a million. Adding to the human resource advantage were the diploma engineers, of which there were generally 50 percent more than there were degree holders, and about 5 million science graduates. This is the dividend earned from half a century's judicious investment in technical and scientific education, something that Nehru was obsessed about.

"What do we do with jobless engineers?" an entire generation had lamented. Suddenly there seemed to be more jobs than engineers. In a campus interview for a job in the technology sector, who is testing whom (recruiter or potential recruit) is sometimes a debatable issue. Even in highly regarded firms like Infosys and TCS, the attrition rate touches 15 percent. And with India's IT-ITES exports scaling up, it is doubtful that there will be fewer jobs than applicants any time in the near future. This is despite new engineering colleges starting up in hundreds and the number of fresh engineering graduates swelling from about 400,000 in 2003–2004 to an estimated 550,000 in 2007–2008. Buoyed by the swelling numbers of engineers in India, Texas Instruments has partnered with more than 450 universities in the country to hone the students' engineering skills before they enter the job market.

There is no country that is in the same league as India as far as the spread and depth of its IT exports are concerned, and none that can produce skilled human resources in such large numbers. The two countries that are usually compared to India are Israel and Ireland. India overwhelms them with its sheer numbers. In 2003, a study estimated that Israel and Ireland had no more than one-tenth of the workers employed by India's software export industry. Nor does either of these countries have any cost advantage to offer. Israeli and Irish software professionals earn many times the wages of their Indian counterparts. India, on the other hand, can safely treble its engineering college seats without any fear of oversupply. India has unmatched headroom for growth.

The Knowledge Society

When the laggard wins the race, the skeptic gnashes his teeth. Initially, some analysts were doubtful whether the Indian IT industry would be able to deliver those services that the West might think too valuable to be offshored to distant Asia. But now the skepticism about the sustainability of the Indian software industry seems to be focused on three deficiencies, from which India will allegedly never be able to escape. First, today its domestic market is weak, thus keeping it excessively dependent on exports and, therefore, subject to the protectionist pressures that build up in the destination countries from time to time. Second, India lacks infrastructure. Finally, the supply of skilled personnel may be adequate in sheer numbers, but there are sometimes questions about their finish and domain knowledge.

Much of the doubt regarding India's future capability arises from a rather limited view of IT and its application. It focuses on the cost advantage that India surely enjoys. But that is only a partial view; the Indian edge comes mostly from the abundance of its talents and its capacity to assimilate technology. It is this advantage that enables Indian IT entrepreneurs to scale up every operation outsourced to them when necessary, to any level that one wishes. I wonder whether global manufacturers can repose the same confidence in other countries that can boast a large population of technically trained personnel. In IT, India has further consolidated its lead by subjecting itself rigorously to global quality standards. India-based centers hold the largest number of quality certifications achieved by any country. As of the end of 2006, more than 400 Indian companies had international quality certificates, with 82 companies certified as SEI CMM Level 5. No other country, including the United States, the issuer country of this certificate, can boast this number.

Behind this large number of quality certificates is an appreciation of India's uniqueness in adding value to a product—not by turning a screw or bringing down a hammer, but by reprogramming a machine so that it functions better, cheaper, or faster. Indian companies are constantly doing this in the most unobtrusive manner. There is invariably an Indian hand in the improvement of a multitude of products and services—whether it be the circuit board of a small MP3 player or the advanced surveillance systems of large public buildings in the West. I was both very amazed and very proud when someone from Fiat showed me the inside of the Italian auto-maker's Alfa Romeo racing car, with its satellite navigation system fully designed by India's very own Wipro Technologies.

The "Indian touch" shows in a large gamut of products and services. Texas Instruments's development center in India, for example, has designed a hybrid mobile chip that is expected to cut the costs of handsets by 40 percent. Motorola's research and development facilities in India helped produce the under-$40 (Rs 1,592) handsets for emerging markets. In a different sphere, India's gaming and animation market is expected to quadruple to $1.3 billion (Rs 51.73 billion) in 2009 as companies tap the country's large pool of low-cost software professionals. The cost of production of a 30-minute animated program in India is about half of that in Korea and Taiwan, and a quarter to a sixth of that in the United States.

Besides, India's domestic IT and ITES market is growing 25 percent annually, in step with the country's integration into the global economy and the spread of e-governance. IT will play a key role in the universalization of education, making governance more transparent and making the law courts easily accessible to the common people. The central government has begun accepting income tax returns filed online, and complex identity-related national citizen databases are in the making.

As India enters a fully technology-driven world, its appetite for IT will be all-embracing—just as human life in the developed economies became driven by electricity in the beginning of the last century. Right now, India is at the threshold of an "IT age," with a quantum jump in its consumption of IT products and services in the offing. India has already made these giant strides with just 5 percent Internet users, compared to about 30 percent in Europe. And even this modest Internet penetration has been possible as a result of the low rates of broadband connection (around $3—Rs 119.5—per month) and affordable PCs priced at $400 (Rs 15,916).

What could have given India its initial advantage in IT? It seems that the answer lies in India's long-established tradition of remembering the canonical texts, including the *Rig-Veda*, believed to have been composed between 1700 and 1100 BC. The nineteenth-century German Indologist Friedrich Max Müller, who translated the *Rig-Veda* from a birch bark manuscript, made an astounding tabulation of the volume of its contents: 1,028 poems; 10,580 verses; 153,826 words. Writing was nearly unknown in India until four centuries before Christ, yet Vedic literature had developed for over a thousand years before that. Max Müller talks of the "Strotriyas" of India, who learned the entire body of Vedic literature from the mouth of their guru and, after a time, taught it to their own pupils. "I have had such students in my room at Oxford, who not only could repeat these [*Rig-Veda*] hymns, but who repeated them with their proper accents (for the Vedic Sanskrit has accents like Greek), nay who, when looking through my printed edition of the *Rig-Veda*, could point out a misprint without the slightest hesitation." In all these centuries, the DNA that enables people to hold, sort, and index information in the mind alone has not changed.

The IT industry has become a big calling card for India, doing for it something much like what the automobile industry did for the United States in the early twentieth century. It used to be said that what was good for General Motors (GM) was good for America. Though this was a good tagline for GM, it also had an element of truth. The automobile industry indeed had a commitment to the United States, creating jobs, paying dividends, and creating the American identity as a technology products leader. To India, the IT industry has contributed all that plus a new image that is easily recognized the world over.

And now, as the country focuses more on trade in knowledge than in skills requiring social accomplishment, such as the services offered from call centers, it will have an even wider scope for looking beyond the smart set in the metropolitan areas—at the talent churning up in the small towns, even the countryside, with the spread of higher education. This will be a golden opportunity for India's IT wizards to overcome their somewhat elitist present identity and to plug the disconnect that their industry at times has with ordinary Indians. IT can mean "India transformed"; it can also mean "ivory tower." It is up to the software gurus of Bangalore and Hyderabad to make their choice.

Chapter 6

The Buzz of Factories

$\mathcal{A}$ visitor to London's Hyde Park cannot help being reminded of the Great Exhibition that Queen Victoria opened there in the Crystal Palace on May 1, 1851. That triumph of prefabricated iron and glass was perhaps put up not very far from the cafeteria at the park's center where the visitor can enjoy her cappuccino, and wonder. Separated from the traffic at Marble Arch or Knightsbridge by many acres of parkland, this is a good place to reflect on the pranks that time plays on national ego.

The 1851 exhibition, with displays ranging from steam hammers and locomotives to camels and elephants and retinues of Asian and African "natives," was, along with the razzmatazz, an imperial display of the British dominance of world industry. This cold and rain-swept island was at that time producing more than half of the world's iron, coal, and cotton cloth. It was only half a century earlier that Britain had beaten France for the economic leadership of Europe, at a time when Europe itself was lagging far behind China and India in manufacturing output. And just 50 years after the exhibition, the center of global industrial dominance was to shift across the Atlantic, to America.

It is important to keep in mind that glories are fleeting before one starts assessing the relative strength of national industrial economies in every age. This is also relevant for placing India on the world industrial map that is unfolding. In 1947, India, like all other preindustrial societies, began its journey as idyllic and poor. Agriculture accounted for about 60 percent of the GDP. Industry's share was a paltry 11 percent in 1950–1951.

Much has changed in the six decades since independence. Agriculture, although still looking big because of the sheer size of the country, has actually been reduced to a tiny, and continually shrinking, 18.5 percent of the GDP. Industry undoubtedly has a larger presence in GDP, about 26 percent in 2006–2007. The obvious question is: what is it that makes up the rest of the GDP?

It is the services sector. From being close to one-fourth of the economy, it has now increased to become more than half of it. From designing aeronautical engines and drug molecules to delivering lunch boxes to office employees, its variety is breathtaking.

The New Frontier

India has no doubt followed an unconventional route to economic growth. In East Asia, growth has been almost entirely industry-driven. Industry accounts for 50 percent of the GDP of Malaysia (2004), 44 percent of that of Thailand, and 46 percent of that of China. India has been late to wake up to the orchestra of "spinning wheels whirled, looms rattled, hammers thumped and needles flew." What has caused this asymmetry? What will it cost us in the future? These are the questions that are worth considering. Taking a dip into the past, one finds a stunning similarity between India's situation now and that of Britain at the turn of the nineteenth century. Just like Britain 200 years ago, India today is at a point of inflection. Its industry has taken off without making an announcement. Even though Englishmen at that time saw their country as a land of bucolic charm, as portrayed in Constable's landscapes, the chimneys of the "satanic mills" were springing up everywhere.

India too is in the midst of a massive transformation from a seemingly agrarian sprawl to a modern industrial state with many postindustrial features. And the takeoff has now begun. The growth of all manufactured goods is up. But what's going up faster than anything else is the gap between what has been forecast and what is actually achieved. Early in 2007, my ministry officials told me that the Index of Industrial Production might go up 11.3 percent, but it increased by 12.5 percent in that period. If steady growth in the production of capital goods (boilers, cranes, and so on) is an indication of an industrial pole vault, such a trend has existed for quite some time now. The growth rate of capital goods each year since 2001–2002 has always been higher than the previous year's rate. It reached 18.2 percent in 2006–2007. And some of the future projections are mind-boggling. A CII-McKinsey report estimates that manufacturing exports from India are likely to grow to $300 billion (Rs 11.94 trillion) in 2015. Of this, $70 to $90 billion (Rs 2.79 trillion to Rs 3.58 trillion, respectively) is expected to come from just four sectors: apparel, auto components, specialty chemicals, and electrical and electronic products.

And the extent to which India is "planning big" is breathtaking:

- In 2006–2007, India produced a modest number of 1.5 million *passenger vehicles*, although this is a long way ahead of the 1980s, when the country made only about 60,000 passenger vehicles in a single year. However, Toyota, Ford, Honda, Mitsubishi, General Motors, China's Chery Automobiles, and the French Renault have now lined up to turn India into a global platform, particularly for small cars. Sales of passenger vehicles are now growing 14 percent annually, but this trot will turn into a gallop with all these investments, with India being projected to produce over 4 million passenger vehicles annually by 2016. The domestic sales orientation of the industry (13 percent exported in 2006–2007) is expected to shift to an export orientation, with 1 million out of 3 million vehicles produced likely to be exported as early as 2012. The Indian market and its auto industry are already the toast of world automakers. It is quite likely that the stars of the international motor shows will soon roll off production lines located not in the United States or Germany or Japan but in Indian cities like Pune or Chennai, one of the fast-growing hubs of the automobile and auto components industry in India.

- In steel, India admittedly still has a long way to go. The country is ranked as only the seventh-largest steel producer against a worldwide demand of approximately 1,200 million metric tons (1,322.7 tons). It took India more than two decades to reach the present production figure, starting from a base of less than 10 million metric tons (11.2 tons). The country consumes only 33 kilograms (72.7 pounds) of steel per capita, compared with 400 kilograms (881.8 pounds) in the developed world and 240 kilograms (529.1 pounds) in China.

    Today India has become the focus of the steel industry globally. With India-born L. N. Mittal's global firm acquiring Europe's Arcelor and many other steelworks worldwide, and the

Indian major Tata Steel taking over the Anglo-Dutch firm Corus, the technology is now within India's grasp. Many new steel plants are under construction, including two by Mittal himself of 12 million metric tons (13.2 tons) capacity each, and another 12-million-metric-ton unit by Korea's POSCO. Indian steel barons are making several outbound investments—in Canada, South Africa, Thailand, Indonesia, and Vietnam. The National Steel Policy, formulated in 2005, modestly calculated production in 2011–2012 at 65 million metric tons (71.7 tons), but we now believe that this figure will be "hugely exceeded." The present tempo of investment envisages production of not less than 120 million metric tons (132.3 tons) in 2015–2016, making India the world's second-largest steel producer, second only to China and ahead of Japan.

- *Auto components* are yet another industry in India that has reached the tipping point. And, like vehicles and steel, its orientation is changing from domestic consumption to export. In 2006–2007, India produced about $15 billion worth of auto components, of which about $3 billion was exported. But Indian component makers have been fast on the uptake and are seeing quantum leaps in exports to the U.S. and European Union (E.U.) markets, past the high accepted quality level (AQL) wall. Indian companies like Bharat Forge, Sundaram Fasteners, and Motherson Sumi have made their way to the premier leagues in the auto components markets of the world. The global carmakers already source sizable shares of engine parts, drive transmission and steering parts, bodies and chassis, equipment, and electrical parts from them.

The "Indian advantage" in this industry stems from the country's sophisticated engineering skills, tested production lines, and competitive costs. Huge investments are being made in this industry at home and abroad. The big car brands are expanding their original equipment manufacturer (OEM) footprint in India, with three-quarters of Indian auto-component exports being bought directly by companies like Ford, BMW, and GM as original equipment. As in many other industries, rising wages and demography may not allow the developed countries to churn out auto components in large volumes any longer. The industry is expected to reach $2 trillion (Rs 79.58 trillion) in 2015. Of this, about 40 percent is likely to be sourced from low-cost countries, with India almost certain to be in the vanguard. Indian auto component manufacturers are projected to export $20 billion (Rs 795.8 billion) worth of products by 2015.

• In the 1970s, India pursued its own drug patent policy, which enabled the *pharmaceutical industry* to keep drug prices low and expand production; but the country remained cut off from the mainstream of innovation. This is no longer the case. Some major firms are setting up "research-based" ventures with Indian companies. Last year, Merck partnered with Advinus Therapeutics, an Indian company, to develop drugs for metabolic disorders, with Merck retaining the right to advance research into late-stage clinical trials. GlaxoSmithKline and Ranbaxy have also teamed up.

There is a lot more headroom, since a full two-thirds of the $9.5 billion (Rs 378.01 billion) global contract clinical research industry is still based in the United States. In the next 10 to 15 years, a third of the world's clinical research will be conducted in India, as a result of a combination of low cost and world-class quality standards. This is a business that will be worth $30 billion (Rs 1.19 trillion) globally by 2010. But India is already a star nation among drug exporters, producing about 22 percent of the world's generic drugs in value terms, and double that share in quantity terms. A new chapter began when the government brought in an amendment to the patent legislation in January

2005, bringing the product (not just the process) within the patent regime.

The products launched since 2005 now account for 12 percent of overall market growth. Foreign direct investment (FDI) in the pharmaceutical sector increased at an astounding 62.6 percent annually in the 2002–2006 period. India now has the highest number of manufacturing plants approved by the U.S. Food and Drug Administration (FDA), second only to the United States itself.

Examples of this kind are abundant. But I think it is necessary at this point to look for the reasons for this burst of industrial activity. The most obvious reason is that India, after many decades of remaining a low-income economy, has at last got the surplus to save and invest. It denotes a qualitative leap in India's capacity to invest. As the Prime Minister's Economic Advisory Council observes in its 2007 report, in an uncharacteristically buoyant tone:

> The strength of domestic conditions supportive of economic growth emanates from the strong investment boom in evidence in recent years. This may be seen from two inter-related facts. First is the big increase in the investment rate, which had stagnated in the 20–25 per cent bracket from the mid-Seventies. In the years after the reforms of 1991, the investment rate between 1997–98 and 2001–02 was 24 per cent on an average. The momentum of investment expansion gathered steam and in 2006–07, it crossed 35 per cent. In every sense, the magnitude of the change in the trajectory of investment is large and significant.

As for the investment rate, India now seems to be entering the zone in which China was placed in the first two years of the millennium (until 2003). Its investment rate was 40 percent of the GDP on average. But the growth story does not end with investment spending. It embraces bank credit to industry, real interest rates, and the efficiency of the capital market. All these factors together—some more and some less—have propelled the entire region of East Asia and China onto a growth path since the 1970s. And now the gale has reached India, with a momentum that may exceed that of all other countries for reasons that are unique to India, in particular its cost-effective production, skilled workforce, and expanding middle class, which is bigger than that of any E.U. country and is still expanding.

Investment in the Indian stock markets has created an extraordinary value over the last six years. Total market capitalization rose from 27 percent of GDP to 92 percent in the period between fiscal years 2001 and 2007. A study conducted by the Boston Consulting Group reveals that a sample of the top 200 Indian companies produced total shareholder return (TSR) of 40 percent, 20 times higher than that of a sample of 1,026 global companies. Analysis shows that better performance on business fundamentals, sales and profit growth, has been the predominant driver of this spectacular growth. Despite the global competition and rising raw material costs, the profitability of the Indian sample set actually increased by 2 percent, and sales growth has been robust. Surely Indian industry has not grown at the cost of profitability. The majority of the top 20 value creators in stock markets are in industrial manufacturing, engineering and construction, materials and commodities, and automotives—not the much-talked-about new knowledge economy and service industries.

India's Advantage

I was curious when Bill Ford, chairman and CEO of Ford Motor Company, said: "This market [India] is critical to our plans for building a Ford Motor Co. for the 21st century." Certainly India is moving out of its decades of economic lethargy, and if things go the right way, it may emerge as a middling economy some day soon. But why is India "critical" to a transnational corporation's future?

I got at least part of the answer when a friend from abroad who has invested in India told me that he had saved a lot on production design and process engineering cost because of the abundance of low-cost, high-quality engineering talent in India. "The boys out here are pretty smart . . . give them a mouse and they'll draw an engine." I found his view entirely supported by Deloitte, a consulting firm, which has even estimated that such savings can be as much as 80 percent compared with plants in developed markets. Prior to 1991, when maintaining a foreign car in India had become painful because the import of spare parts was not allowed or was too costly, workshops with their own lathe machines that could forge the components of even the top luxury car models mushroomed in every Indian city. On the other hand, the molecules that go into the aspirin tablet might be a Western invention, but, since the Indian drug companies were free to produce these molecules any way they wanted, it was their prerogative and their achievement to make the tablets at the lowest cost. India's capacity to assimilate, synthesize, and modernize is infinite; this is India's genius.

Added to this is India's high capital productivity. Indians are generally frugal with capital. Although they may be ostentatious on social occasions—family weddings, for instance—they tend to be extremely cost-conscious in business spending; their businesses are usually great sticklers for the norms of debt/equity ratios, and loan default is a matter of honor. Also, Indians squeeze the highest return from every rupee invested in their enterprises.

McKinsey has an interesting study of India's cost advantage. According to this study, if the cost of setting up a plant in the United States is taken as 100, the cost in India would be 68. Significantly, while the cost of equipment for the plant in the United States has been put at 60, in India it is only 39. For a medium-voltage switching device plant, if the cost in Europe is 100, it will be 67 in India. For making components of that switching device, the ratio is a steeper 100:59. As would be expected, India's cost advantage is more pronounced at the lower end of the value chain, but its rise implies that it is becoming competitive in value-added products as well.

Indian business owners' penchant for using capital efficiently shows in many ways. They are adept at using plants and machinery long after they are, legally speaking, fully depreciated, and will postpone their replacement for as long as possible. They are careful about use of raw material and generally keep an eagle eye on inventory. They cut costs but do not shy away from commitment. There are a very few instances of global importers complaining about Indian companies having reneged on promise of delivery on specious grounds, but they are the exceptions. The Indian capital efficiency arises out of not just cost saving but working hard. India works 24/7/365—if shipments have to go out, they have to go out.

Accumulation of capital for investment is not a sufficient prerequisite for high industrial growth. It is necessary for the capital to be efficiently employed. The capacity to do this is embedded in the genes of Indian businesspeople. A somewhat xenophobic businessman friend who was opposed to the 1991 reform often told me, only half in jest, "The multinationals are said to have deep pockets, but we Indians generally wear trousers that have no pockets at all." Today, his sons (and heirs) have diversified the family's business. Some of their companies are giving their multinational rivals a run for their money. That my skeptical friend's son has beaten financially better endowed rivals shows that Indians tend to use capital more efficiently than others.

A back-of-the-envelope calculation will reinforce this point about India's capital efficiency. Over the 1995–2005 decade, India's average annual GDP growth rate of 6 percent was supported by an investment rate of 22–23 percent of GDP. China has seven times more FDI and eight times more exports, but only 1.3 percent more GDP growth.

India's high efficiency of capital use plays on some of the country's traditional social values. In India, defaulting on a loan involves the honor, or *izzat*, of the individual or the clan. This is one reason why India has been able to hold down its banks' ratio of net nonperforming assets to total assets to an enviably healthy level of 0.7 in 2005–2006. So it is India's social attitude to capital, its cost advantages, and its rising productivity that have qualified it to attract investment from home and abroad.

When this social attitude is extended to public action, it can hamper growth at times. For example, the condition of the country's infrastructure is woefully inadequate. Rather than being put down to a general apathy, this is ascribed to the collective trait of being cautious with money, spending only one dollar when two dollars are preferable and never the other way round. However, in the past two years or so, infrastructure is the buzz, with billions of dollars worth of new investments flowing into railways, roads, power, ports, airports, and urban transportation. Investment in infrastructure also fuels the growth of industry, including high-tech industry. The new generation passenger trains that are being planned will have top speeds nearing 300 kilometers per hour (187 miles per hour). It is through superior infrastructure that the seeds of superior technology are sown, as in Japan in the 1960s (when the bullet train was introduced) or as is happening in China at present.

Home and the World

This is the title of a novel by Rabindranath Tagore (1861–1941), nationalist and Bengali writer, who in 1913 was the first Asian to get the Nobel Prize in literature. Set in the early twentieth century, it is the story of a wealthy and liberal man's abhorrence of an excess of nationalism sliding into xenophobia.

In a way, Indian industry is a fine balance between the "home" and the "world." The growth of India's industry is being propelled by its familiarity with the developed markets in the West, just as its IT skills developed as a result of the exposure of its engineers and technology experts to Western markets. In India, the world is firmly implanted in the home. When it comes to business practices, India is one of the fastest learners from the West, second only to Japan, perhaps. Most of its leading business houses publish their accounts following both the conventional system and the American accounting norm, GAAP (Generally Accepted Accounting Principles). The banks follow the same prudent norms as those in Europe or America.

India's film industry, Bollywood, nowadays draws its revenues of about $1.5 billion (Rs 59.69 trillion) almost equally from the domestic and foreign markets. The PricewaterhouseCoopers Global Entertainment and Media Outlook has ranked India as the fastest-growing market for entertainment and media, with a cumulative annual growth rate (CAGR) of 18.5 percent. And equally interesting is the evolving versatility of India's drug industry, which offers both the lifesaving drugs needed by India's poor and the lifestyle drugs of the rich in the West.

A fine example of how overseas markets and consumer preferences have spurred Indian industry comes from Tirupur, an obscure town in the south Indian state of Tamil Nadu. In the 1930s, knitwear units appeared for the first time in that area, maybe because of a drop in the price of the imported knitting machines. Ten years later, as labor militancy was on the rise in the south, Tirupur, then a nondescript town, proved to be an island of stability. Thus most of the knitwear units located there, making it the location of a cluster of knitted textile firms. The units, however, were composite, with little scope for division of labor and thus for honing specialized skills. This was all right as long as Tirupur served only the domestic market, which was limited in both size and variety. However, in 1978, an Italian garment importer visited Tirupur to buy white T-shirts. He was most impressed by the job that the workers, who were manufacturing garments for merchant exporters, were doing. Following his lead, many other European buyers came to Tirupur, and the little knitting town woke up to the presence of the European market.

The consequent demand for volume and quality brought about a fundamental change in Tirupur's business pattern. From the confines of a factory shed, all garment manufacturing activities were outsourced to neighboring units specializing in knitting, dyeing and bleaching, fabric printing, stitching, embroidery, compacting, and calendaring. It was exactly as Adam Smith described the division of operations in a pin manufacturer between drawing the wire, cutting, head fitting, and sharpening. From then on, Tirupur became an export hub. A. Sakhtivel, who heads the Tirupur Exporters Association, claims that he's following a road map that will take exports to $6 billion (Rs 238.8 billion) in 2012. He is anything but overoptimistic. Tirupur has on its client list every top name in the garment trade: Nike, Cutter & Buck, Adidas, Tommy Hilfiger, Arrow, and so on. It has every chain store sourcing from it, including Wal-Mart, C&A, and Mother Care.

But, more importantly, Tirupur has an astounding ability to recognize the swings in consumer taste in the Western market and to respond to them immediately. It is a prime example of export-led growth achieved purely through the entrepreneurs' initiative, without any government intervention. When I was textiles minister (1995–1996), the exporters in Tirupur invited me to tour their facilities and address a meeting. I still remember my experience and how I began my speech: "You people are so smart and so efficient, you don't need a textile minister within 10 miles. In fact, I don't think you need the government. But the government needs you, of course!"

Knowledge of overseas markets and consumer preferences has worked effectively in categories where it is important to know what the customer likes to have. This is happening in businesses that are fragmented, like textiles or gems and jewelry, or that are on the cutting edge, such as biotechnology. On the one hand, India has an 8 percent share of the world export of jewelry, which is rising; on the other, it makes more than a fifth of the world's generic drugs. India is engaging the interest of the global customer.

The textiles and clothing industry, which provides direct employment to 38 million people, has been on a downswing since the 1980s, as it remained protected by tariffs and the quota system, which limited India's ability to export. However, globalization of trade has now robbed it of its tariff protection, and the abolition of the quota system has put this industry's exports into high gear; they were worth $20 billion (Rs 795.8 billion) last year and are projected to rise 22 percent a year until 2012, hitting $55 billion (Rs 2.2 trillion) that year.

India looks like the perfect volume player in textiles. It has approximately 20 percent of the world's spinning capacity and about 35 percent of its weaving. This, combined with the vast pool of low-cost workers, should make India a leading player. But there have been interesting new developments. There is a sudden spurt in collaboration between Indian and foreign textile companies. There is a relentless melding now between the Indian providers of materials and fashion industry leaders from abroad. It is again the osmosis of knowledge at work.

This is also happening in gems and jewelry, with the 300,000 traditional jewelers going through a phase of cultural reinvention of their skills as multinational luxury brands seem set to unfurl their banners following my ministry's decision to allow FDI of up to 51 percent in single-brand retail stores. Many of these transnational corporations have been sourcing cut and polished diamonds and ornamental gold items from the Indian jewelers for years. Now it is time for them to set up joint ventures and start the exchange of knowledge.

Biotechnology, however, is one sector in which India is on a somewhat different platform—as an advanced player in the knowledge league. Biotechnology is a *science* that has been maturing into a *business* over the past 10 years or so, and this sector in India seems to be driven by the same enterprise and innovation as its Western counterparts. The industry is set to reach the critical volume of $5 billion (Rs 198.95 billion) in the middle of the 2006–2015 decade, which has been pronounced the "decade of Asia" for biotechnology.

This is an area in which India has an enviable pool of researchers. It already enjoys a high level of compliance with internationally harmonized standards like Good Laboratory Practices (GLP), Good Manufacturing Practices (GMP), and Good Clinical Practices (GCP). It has an IPR regime that is rated among the strongest in the developing economies. An Ernst and Young study has named India as one of the five emerging biotech leaders in the Asia Pacific region, along with Japan, Singapore, Taiwan, and South Korea.

Biotechnology is a bit of a business in transition, somewhat like what telecommunications became with the advent of first wireless technology and then the Internet. Medical researchers believe that, in the not too distant future, they will be able to use technologies derived from adult and embryonic stem cell research to treat a host of diseases, including cancer and Type 1 diabetes mellitus. Their success may decide the future course of biotechnology. But, regardless of its future course, India will consolidate its strength in this sector because of its long exposure to Western medical education and the consequent abundant availability of the ultimate capital in the knowledge business—the human mind.

Blackboard and Business

In India, the individual entrepreneur is free to raise capital for his intended business in any way he wants, whether by borrowing or by surrendering his mortgage, but the development of the human capital he needs depends on decisions taken almost entirely in the public domain. Primary education is largely funded by the state, as is higher education to a great extent. For human capital, size matters. Many countries have produced legendary scholars and have been responsible for a great many innovations. But industrial preeminence cannot be sustained over time without the strength of numbers. (Britain was an exception, its preeminence having been leveraged by its empire.)

India's core strength as a rising industrial power resides in the approximately 2.6 million to 2.9 million university students who graduate each year. The number is awe-inspiring. It is this human capital that has put India at the forefront of the new wave of industrialization based on an easy, inexpensive, and quick dispersal of knowledge across the globe. Nothing like this has happened in the past. In the nineteenth century, the British jealously guarded ownership of the three pillars of Victorian wealth creation: the steamship, the railway, and the electric telegraph. But the world has indeed been "flattened" so much in the intervening centuries that no knowledge breakthrough can remain under wraps for too long.

There is a general misconception, though, about the linkage between industrial growth and the spread of high-level scientific and technical education. John Kenneth Galbraith, in his much-acclaimed book *The Affluent Society*, showed that the harbingers of the Industrial Revolution in Britain were fairly ordinary peasants and mechanics, far from the rocket scientists that many people later imagined them to be. John Kay, the man behind the flying shuttle, was a weaver, as was James Hargreaves of spinning jenny fame.

But times have changed, and so has industry's need. It is not possible to run a manufacturing business in any corner of the world today with employees who have the same level of education that the workers in Henry Ford's early automobile factory had. There is a need today for high-level institutions and their products. India is, of course, proud of its IITs (Indian Institutes of Technology), which are seven in number at the moment (this should become 15 soon), and its six Indian Institutes of Management (IIMs). Even adding to these the likes of the National Institute of Design and the seven National Institute of Fashion Technology, however, the list of elite institutes still seems to be limited for a country of India's dimensions.

In the 2005 *London Times* Higher Education Supplement (THES), India's IITs were ranked third among technical institutes globally, after the Massachusetts Institute of Technology (MIT) and the University of California at Berkeley. But behind these elite institutions are a myriad of other colleges and institutes of equally fine caliber, and at a shop-floor level, there are hundreds of ITIs (industrial training institutes) producing skilled technicians in every district.

The next big push—an absolute priority—must be in higher education. Since business is hungry for skilled labor, it might take some initiative here, as well.

From academic centers, the prime requirement of business is high-quality research. In OECD (Organization for Economic Cooperation and Development) countries, 60 percent of basic research is sourced from academic institutions. However, the research output of Indian institutes of higher learning is relatively low by international standards. According to the Institute for Scientific Information (ISI), India's share of the world publication of research papers stood at 2 percent in 2003. A deficit is also evident in the gross enrollment ratio for all kinds of higher education; India's level is just about 10 percent, whereas the current general pattern is 15 percent for the lower-middle-income countries, 26 percent for the upper-middle-income countries, and 62 percent for countries in the high-income group. So business should also start coming closer to the blackboard. This is in fact happening, as the following examples indicate:

- The number of *engineering colleges*, which stood at 669 in 1999–2000, had climbed to 1,478 in 2005–2006, a jump of 121 percent in six years, with 88 percent of the increase funded by the private sector.

- The number of *pharmacy* schools rose from 204 in 1999–2000 to 629 in 2005–2006, a 208 percent jump, with 94 percent private-sector financing.

- The number of *architecture* schools rose from 47 to 70 in the same period, a 51 percent jump, with 67 percent private financing.

- The number of *business management* schools went from 682 to 1,052, an increase of 55 percent, with 64 percent private financing.

- Finally, the number of schools of *medicine* went from 174 to 229, a 32 percent increase, with 46 percent of the cost being borne by the private sector.

It is evident that the private sector has taken the initiative and has begun to look at higher education as a supply-side challenge. However, elementary education is exclusively in the state's domain. India has already achieved 70 percent literacy, and things will improve as the economy expands and tax revenues increase. In the past, these schools suffered because of inadequate public spending. Since 2004, the Indian government has introduced an education tax exclusively for financing universal elementary education. With improvements in public finance, and with education being seen as a precondition for a decent livelihood, it is likely that there will be an increase in enrollments at all levels of education—primary, secondary, and tertiary—and this will bring India closer to the much-needed *knowledge dividend.*

Past records alone do not provide a reliable picture of how industry will develop in the future. In a land in which several paradigm shifts are taking place simultaneously, as in India, the future will be far from a replication of the past. It can be felt only on the basis of the dynamic of the present. The question that follows is: what can fuel India's sustained industrial growth?

A nation's industry improves only as fast as it can raise its productivity level. Rapid growth in a nation's labor force and capital stock does not by itself lead to improved living standards. This also requires improvement in total factor productivity (TFP), which is a rough aggregate of the productivities of all the factors of production, especially labor and capital. It is unfair to hold that China has vastly improved its citizens' standard of living only *because* of regimented labor and high investments. What has boosted its TFP has been the universal and compulsory nine years of school education, which has virtually eradicated illiteracy and has created a responsive industrial labor force.

India has not been oblivious to the dire necessity of improving the standards of general education, with technical training as its focus. Since independence, there have been schemes to provide vocational training for craftspersons in as many as 107 different trades. The training period varies from six months to three years. Since 2005, the training system in these schools, known as Industrial Training Institutes (ITIs), has undergone a huge overhaul. The project, assisted by the World Bank, is designed to create skilled workers for modern industries. Organized in clusters and located close to selected industries, these institutes will provide the trained workforce that no industry, however state-of-the-art and automated, can do without.

The most significant point is that India's multiplying armies of industrial workers will remain young for a longer time than those of any other country, including China. They will bring to India a nonstop gain in labor productivity. This can translate into a basket of gains, like globally competitive costs of production and un-matchable volumes. Such a situation, which is quite logical, will make absolutely believable the utterance of Matti Pietarinen, deputy director general of the Ministry of Trade and Industry in Finland, the country that gave the world the Nokia cell phone, that "I can foresee a day when Finland could begin importing mobile phones from India." By a grand reversal of fortune, India may then be called both the "workshop of the world" and its "back office," the two rolled into one.

Chapter 7

At India's Service

In the heart of Delhi is a cavernous, imperial-style building—designed by Edwin Lutyens, the British architect of the 1920s—called Udyog Bhawan (literally, Industry House). It houses India's Ministry of Commerce and Industry, and since the summer of 2004, it has been my place of work. Walking into the building today—or, indeed, even three years ago—one is struck by a sense of irony. As India's economy has become progressively deregulated and expanded, as the country's trade has increased and its manufacturing has gathered pace, Udyog Bhawan's responsibilities have been redefined. It has become less crowded and populated—literally—than it was at an earlier time. This is a happy sign of change. The extent of crowding of a regulatory ministry's building is an important index of how liberated an economy is. If businesspeople, industrial barons, and foreign investors are hanging around some government office instead of being in the market, assessing investment decisions and doing deals, then there is something wrong somewhere.

My first visit to the building was to a very different Udyog Bhawan in a very different India. Close to 40 years ago, accompanying an uncle who was trying to get permission to import new machines for his light engineering industrial unit, I got an eyewitness look at the travails of what we today call small and medium enterprises (SME). My uncle went from room to room, door to door, not forgetting to almost obsequiously thank even the man at the reception desk who perfunctorily wrote out an entry pass that allowed us to get into the hallowed precincts.

Udyog Bhawan's corridors were busy. One could see, and even recognize, well-known magnates, businessmen, exporters, importers, lobbyists, middlemen, license seekers, and quota hunters. About a year into my current term as minister, an old friend from Kolkata—a member of one of India's oldest and most established business families—met me at a social gathering and said, "I understand Udyog Bhawan looks very different these days. It's been cleaned and spruced up, I hear. I must come over one of these days. I haven't visited that building in years."

My eyes lit up—not because I was responsible for Udyog Bhawan's interior decor, but because a leading businessman had frankly admitted that he no longer needed to spend hours meeting the "right people" in a building that was once familiar ground for him. This is, of course, not because of just one minister or one government. It is the result of a process—one that is still continuing—that began in 1991 and has been sustained by many of my distinguished predecessors in the Ministry of Commerce and Industry. Today, as I once told a political colleague, only half in jest, there are more people behind the counter at the entrance than in front of it. If I can leave the ratio even more skewed, I will leave Udyog Bhawan a satisfied man.

Rereading the Trade Winds

Along with the hardware, the software at Udyog Bhawan was also ripe for an upgrade. As tariffs tumbled, domestic industry became vulnerable to external competition. There was then really no option; domestic industry had to import plant and equipment and the latest technology in order to modernize. This was the only way it could compete effectively. Further, those entrepreneurs who saw business opportunities overseas also needed to modernize to make their products competitive as exports. We now required a rethinking of our strategy, a sort of second-generation idea of external trade management. Traditionally, Indian governments had had a conservative view of trade. Exports were essentially the part of local production that was not consumed by the domestic economy, imports were frowned upon, and accumulating dollars for the sake of accumulating dollars was the big, overriding theme. Obviously, this outlook would no longer do.

There had to be a renewed thrust toward the export of goods and services—there were new markets and new products that India and Indian companies had left unexplored. Imports were not necessarily bad, especially if what was being brought in was new technology, semifinished goods, and raw materials that Indian factories could add value to and then, in turn, sell to the rest of the world. Finally, in a country with such grinding poverty and high unemployment, trade could not be an end in itself. It had to be a means of economic growth and societal development. The focus had to be on job creation—just as it had been in China or the

Asian Tigers, for example—and not just on shoring up the Reserve Bank of India's dollar reserves, desirable as that objective might be.

If all of that was the "commerce end" of my job, the "industry end" was to promote policies that made Indian manufacturers globally competitive and also to draw in more foreign investment. To be fair, Indian industry had taken some steps in this direction, as slowly but surely the realization was seeping in that producing only slightly better products than your neighbor and living happily in a cosseted local market would no longer be sufficient. If you wanted to export, your goods would have to be export-worthy and internationally acceptable. You had to shape up before you could ship out. That was the logic of globalization.

A second goal was making India a more attractive destination for investment. In the initial years after the reform in 1991, India had been unusual. Its capital markets had attracted substantial amounts of foreign institutional investment (FII), but the amount of foreign direct investment (FDI) was relatively small. But today, according to an A. T. Kearney report, India has displaced the United States as the second most favored destination for foreign direct investment, after China.

Much of India's rising profile as a destination for FDI is the result of the post-1991 improvements in its international competitiveness, which qualify it as one of the active gateways to global trade. But India has to climb several more notches up the competitive ladder if it wishes to match its East Asian peers like South Korea and Thailand, not to mention the Western countries. There are, of course, some economies for which FDI does not really matter, as the sheer size of their workforce and their macroeconomic weight can make up for other deficits. India does have size, but its investment resources are limited. Therefore, to sustain a high growth rate, that growth must be substantially fueled by FDI.

It is pertinent here to take a quick look at the indicators of competitiveness, or, in other words, the factors that determine a country's ranking on the "global competitiveness index." The indicators range from the quality of the country's institutions, infrastructure, macroeconomy, health, and education to such determinants of competitiveness as market efficiency, technological readiness, business sophistication, and innovation. Each of these elements is quantifiable and indexable. India ranks highest among the BRIC countries—Brazil, Russia, India, and China—in competitiveness. In the early 1990s, India placed nowhere in a ranking of global competitiveness. This showed in the trickles that arrived as FDI. The rise of India in the last 10 years is evident in the GCI ranking, and so is its ability to attract investments.

The most significant indicator of global competitiveness is macroeconomic stability. My optimism on this score rests on the ability of India's institutions, notably the polity and the bureaucracy, to offer a solution to the problem of the ballooning deficits. The fiscal deficit of the federal government alone exceeded 6 percent of the GDP three times between 1990–1991 and 2002–2003. The combined gross fiscal deficit of the state governments and the central government even reached a high of 9.93 percent of the GDP in 2001–2002, causing a recurring threat to macroeconomic stability. The government was forced to augment the money supply by crowding out private borrowers, with consequent deleterious effect on demand and price.

However, the Parliament passed a Fiscal Reform and Budget Management Act (FRBMA) that came into force in July 2004. It calls for, among other things, a phased reduction in both the revenue deficit and the fiscal deficit, with the latter becoming less than 3 percent of the GDP before the end of the 2008–2009 financial year. So far the effect of the FRBMA has been spectacular. The central government's fiscal deficit was 3.7 percent of the GDP in 2006–2007, while that of the state governments was another 2.7 percent. With nearly all state governments having passed their own FRBMA, its success is a glowing tribute to the power of India's democracy.

However, the second-generation reform is also aiming at all aspects of governance, the government being "the institution that fixes the pipes." If the reform of 1991 has taught India to improve its markets, the present and future reforms will lead the country on to make its institutions work better.

Reform in India has now entered a complex phase in which strong steps need to be taken to maintain the pace of growth, This, in turn, calls for not only improving productivity and employment but also making the infrastructure available to absorb the demand for industry and its corollary, growth. The country has witnessed inflationary pushes with the first wave of growth. To keep prices under control, infrastructure must be available to propel growth and consumption to newer heights. Also, restructuring of existing assets is necessary to keep the costs competitive.

India has much wealth that is lying unproductive in the country, and these assets have to be made productive. If failed businesses could be wound up easily, making the exit of capital as easy as its entry, entrepreneurs would have fewer inhibitions about investing in new businesses or restructuring old ones. And that would create not only more jobs than the ones lost to closure but also a greater variety of jobs, more suitable to the millions of youngsters with the up-to-date skills relevant to today's technology and needs. These jobs can accommodate a large range of skill sets. However, the state in India cannot go about correcting such distortions with a sledge-hammer. A politician who believes in economic reform faces a challenge and a dilemma, but not an insurmountable one. The situation calls for credible and clear communication of the benefits of economic change and also for educating voters about the realities of globalization, rather than focusing on its imagined perils.

Generally, it takes about a decade after economic reforms take place for serious investors to gain sufficient confidence in the credibility and durability of a country's policy course to put their money into that country. Take China as an example. Between 1985 and 1995, its FDI inflows totaled $11.7 billion. In 1997, they jumped to about $45 billion, and by 2006, they had swelled to approximately $60 billion. Clearly 1997 was something of an inflection point for FDI flows into China. In 2004, India was awaiting its inflection point. This was to come in 2006–2007, when FDI inflows tripled from the previous year and reached $19.5 billion (Rs 775.91 billion). In the first 13 years of economic reform (1991–2004), India saw FDI worth $35 billion (Rs 1.39 trillion) come in. In the next three years (2004–2007), that number was almost equaled and another $34 billion (Rs 1.36 trillion) arrived.

Even if a gradual rise in FDI was in the cards anyway, an exponential leap—a growth in geometric rather than arithmetic progression—required more than just passive patience. It required aggressively opening up various sectors of the economy to FDI. In 2006, for instance, tea plantations (producing a commodity that is almost an Indian trademark) and greenfield airports (a "strategic asset" that to an earlier generation would have been unimaginable outside government control) were opened up to 100 percent FDI, as were mining rights for India's gold, silver, and mineral resources.

Decisions on FDI sometimes involve an interplay of complex issues, such as the consequences of foreign investment in retail. In India, about 96 percent of retail trade is in the unorganized sector and only 4 percent in the organized sector. Allowing global retail chains untrammeled and instant access to the Indian market would entail an intricate matrix of challenges and opportunities for Indian labor that would have to be politically weighed and socially measured.

Exports Equal Employment

Three months after I became the minister of commerce and industry, I was required to make what was probably going to be the most important policy announcement of my term: crafting a Foreign Trade Policy for 2004–2009. Two broad goals were enunciated:

• Doubling India's percentage share of global merchandise trade within five years. (In fact, we doubled India's exports in just three years, from $63 billion (Rs 2.5 trillion) in 2004 to $126 billion (Rs 5 trillion) in 2007, signifying a growth of 25 percent every year.)

• Using trade as an instrument for stimulating economic activity and creating jobs. This would require freeing industry and entrepreneurship from controls, simplifying procedures, bringing down transaction costs, and facilitating India's development as a global hub for manufacturing, trade, and services. It would include an emphasis on the export of agricultural products (like fruits, flowers, and vegetables) and handicrafts and hand-loomed products, in addition to the traditional export powerhouses such as leather and footwear and gems and jewelry. These were sectors that had the potential to make a genuine dent in the unemployment figures.

In short, we were going to use trade to fight poverty. Could this be done? To be sure, we had our share of doubting Thomases. In 2005, my ministry commissioned a report by Research and Information System for Developing Countries (RIS), a Delhi-based economic think tank, that demonstrated that for every additional $1 billion (Rs 39.8 billion) of exports, India would generate 125,000 direct and 100,000 indirect jobs. Based on these figures, the Ministry of Commerce and Industry has helped create 14 million additional jobs, about 8 million direct and 6 million indirect, in the period 2004–2007, the most by any ministry in the government ever. More important, it has demonstrated the direct causal relationship between an open economy, high growth, more trade, and jobs and development.

None of this would have been possible without an energetic response from Indian industry, which took on the challenges of stepping up quantitative growth and enhancing quality with determination and decisiveness. The prime minister set up the National Manufacturing Competitive Council as a facilitative body. This was a genuine partnership between government and industry. Industrial growth touched 11.6 percent for 2006–2007; the average growth rate for 2004–2007 was 8.8 percent. Most heartwarming was the resurgence in Indian manufacturing. The manufacturing sector grew at an average of 9.6 percent a year in 2004–2007. In India's eleventh Five-Year Plan period (2007–2012), it is projected to grow at 12 percent a year.

This endeavor will, of course, mean more trade, more exports, and more jobs. The RIS study estimated that in 2009–2010, India's exports would be worth $165 billion (Rs 6.6 trillion) and would have provided an increment of 12.8 million direct jobs and 10.2 million indirect jobs within five years. Going by what has already been achieved, those may well turn out to have been cautious underestimates.

The Patent Pill

India's industrial and manufacturing renaissance represents a new paradigm. In the various models of economic development in the past century, three broad-brush phases can be detected. The first was the colonial mode of development. Large parts of Latin America, Africa, and Asia, including India, provided the raw materials and the raw muscle power needed to extract these materials—say, iron ore or coal. The finished articles were manufactured in the colonizing country. The second model was largely a postwar phenomenon and was built on public investments in heavy industry, which led to mass manufacture. Variations on this model, with different degrees of technology and efficiency, can be found in Germany, in Russia, and, most recently, in China.

India is at the cusp of the second and third models, not just optimizing the best practices of the earlier models but moving on to what are really "next practices." India is building a knowledge-based industrial setup. Its factories are not sweatshops; they are designed to be run by sophisticated programs. The sinews of the "new" Indian industry are respect for knowledge, knowledge systems, and knowledge protection. In short, India cannot do without a modern and credible patent and intellectual property rights regime. Indeed, India is so conscious of the need to adhere to its commitments in this regard that counterfeiting of brands— garments, watches, and electronic goods, for instance—has been severely curtailed, if not almost eliminated, through governmental enforcement and the law courts.

It was the patent issue that, in November and December of 2004, posed my first major political challenge as commerce and industry minister. In 1995, India had signed the Trade Related Intellectual Property Rights (TRIPs) Agreement as part of the larger document establishing the World Trade Organization (WTO). Under this agreement, India promised to adhere to a timetable for bringing its intellectual property laws into conformity with TRIPs' demands. It committed itself to providing product patent protection in all fields of technology after January 1, 2005. In real terms, this meant the extension of product patent protection to drugs, foods, and chemicals. Other products were already covered by India's patent provisions, which had been written into the law from its very inception.

In the winter of 2004, the Congress-led coalition government was barely six months old. It was dependent in Parliament on support from the Left Front, a conglomeration of four Marxist parties that had consistently opposed India's membership in the WTO.

The Communist parties suggested numerous amendments to the proposed law and openly charged the government with giving in to provisions that would increase the cost of medicines and health care in the country.

The weeks that followed were tense. If the amendments did not go through, the consequences would be colossal. India would be in breach of its WTO commitments. The intellectual property regime in India would come under a cloud, affecting investor confidence and jeopardizing many of the assumptions about industrial growth and exports that had been made when the Foreign Trade Policy was announced in August 2004. Jobs in export-oriented companies would be lost, as trade sanctions would inevitably follow; this would lead to another domestic crisis. Most of all, the credibility of India's reform process, assiduously built since the summer of 1991, would be severely damaged if the amendments to the patent law did not go through.

The amendments to the Patent Act were promulgated by an ordinance in December 2004 to meet the January 1 deadline, as Parliament was not in session at that time. They had to be validated during the next session of Parliament, and the political negotiations and tightrope walking soon began. The left, of course, attacked the bill; one of its members even called it "neocolonial." Interestingly, there was even a claim in Parliament that the United Nations had warned India that the proposed amendments to the Patents Act would have a "devastating impact on the people of this country."

The proposed legislation also allowed for patentability of computer programs if these had technical applications for industry and in combination with hardware. This provision would have implications for India's software industry. During the consultation process involving the political parties and other stakeholders, several modifications were made to the amendments, including deletion of the clarificatory provision on software patents. It was my duty as commerce and industry minister to tell the country that the TRIPs Agreement gave India as many advantages as it did problems. It was not that India was giving away everything and gaining nothing.

In my reply to the debate in the Lok Sabha (lower house of Parliament), I pointed out that the new law also gave intellectual property protection to Indian scientists and technicians and would allow them to "create capital out of their intellect and technical knowledge." I spoke of India's burgeoning pharmaceutical exports and its new emphasis on R&D in a host of fields, including drugs and medicines: "The new reality is that Indian scientists are ready to face the challenge of a post-patent era; Indian companies have over the past few years invested heavily in technology and research infrastructure. Are we not to back our own companies?"

It was a battle between India's past and its future. The bill was passed; the future won.

Diplomacy, Davos/Commerce Style

The WTO has been a familiar battleground in intense negotiation and in shaping a compromise or finding a modus vivendi. So much of modern economic management is actually another facet of diplomacy that it sometimes makes me wonder how the world saw the two fields—economic engagement and diplomacy/international relations—as two distinct, hermetically sealed domains even 20 years ago.

Trade has become the new currency of diplomacy. In the past, whenever Indian dignitaries visited a foreign country, the must-meet list began and ended with politicians, with a few newspaper editors included. But now, with every VIP visit, the simultaneous arrival of a planeload of "captains of industry" is de rigueur. The composition of the entourage of incoming prime ministers and presidents has also undergone a dramatic change. Gone are the strategic and political advisors, and even the cultural troupes. Visiting heads of states or governments would rather arrive with delegations of business leaders, making career diplomats look somewhat diminutive, in importance at least. Trade was the sauce of diplomacy even in the past, but now it appears to have become the main course.

Quite a few countries, such as Brazil and Australia, have merged the trade and foreign ministries into one entity. Whether India too requires a convergence of foreign policy and strategic imperatives is an open issue. Activating Indian embassies as important players in export promotion was a key innovation of the foreign trade policy of 2004. In my job, brand promotion is an imperative. The only difference is that one is not promoting an ordinary brand—a company or a soft drink—but instead a mega-brand called India: a whole country, a full society, a buzzing universe of a billion energized minds. You must convey your message—attempt your brand positioning—with subtlety and improvisation.

Sometimes it takes a blockbuster move to announce your brand's arrival. For India, this happened at the World Economic Forum (WEF) meeting in Davos, Switzerland, in January 2006. The theme for the year was "India Everywhere"; driven substantially by private business houses and associations, with the government providing only backup support, it showcased the dazzling strengths and opportunities that made India such a sought-after prize among emerging economies. To many people—including me—it also emphasized, once and for all, that the India story was unstoppable.

It was at Davos in 2005 that Klaus Schwab, executive chairman of the WEF, told me that he wanted to make India the theme for the following year's event. He sensed that India had reached the takeoff point and that the WEF couldn't postpone the "India year" any longer. I jumped at the offer. The positive momentum generated by such a recognition and the staging of such an event would be incalculable. An India-centric WEF would achieve more than a million dollars of advertising time on every leading media network.

Schwab wanted Prime Minister Manmohan Singh, as the architect and most respected face of the new Indian economy, to come to Davos in 2006. I conveyed this to the prime minister, but he shook his head: "No, I've done this in my time. Now I want others to do it." I knew what the prime minister was trying to do: he was trying to delink process from personality. He was trying to say that the phenomenon of India's economic rise is more important than which face represents it at what time. Finally, he wrote to Schwab, apologizing for his absence and saying, "I've sent you my best team."

Anyone who has attended an Indian wedding will tell you that few people can put on a show the way Indians can. Davos was just such an extravaganza. More than 100 political, government, business, and civil society leaders flew into Switzerland from India. Three union ministers and three state chief ministers participated. Indian food and wines, music and dance, art and pashmina stoles, an "India hour" at Davos's bars—India was truly everywhere. As an Australian acquaintance waved and told me, "It's the Indian takeover, mate."

I wish I could have been a part of all that jazz. I was rather busy with the business side of things, participating in the 12 India-focused sessions and some of the 60 other sessions at the WEF that year. What gratified me was seeing the list of requests for meetings with the Indian minister for commerce and industry and looking at the missed-call register on my cell phone. It just never ended! It was impossible to honor every request. Obviously, these people—CEOs, government leaders, VIPs, very VIPs, and very, very VIPs—weren't calling me because they thought I was an engaging conversationalist. They were calling to talk to India, to an ambassador of the world's most exciting economy. It was my proudest hour; it was also my most humbling moment.

India—*my* India—was right up there: with the stars, knocking on heaven's door.

Chapter

8

The Challenge of Global Trade

For me it will remain an exit to remember. On June 30, 2006, I, as the representative of the Indian government at a crucial WTO meeting in Geneva, left in the middle of the talks. The world media promptly interpreted this as a protest against the West's policy of heavily subsidizing its farmers in order to keep the agricultural produce of developing countries out of the lucrative international markets. The media may have overreacted, but they were right in identifying the fundamental issue causing the impasse in the Doha negotiations.

Disagreement in trade talks is a part of life. It is not quite like foreign policy disputes based on national hubris, which were the hallmark of "great game" diplomacy from Bismarck to Kissinger. Instead, in negotiations over tariffs, subsidies, or market access, there may be a stalemate not because one of the countries, or a group of them, is intransigent but because what appears to one side to be fair trade may not seem fair to the other. And there may be logic on both sides. But on that day, I had mixed feelings, self-confidence blended with a large dose of dejection. India was a founder member of the GATT (General Agreement on Tariffs and Trade) and an ardent advocate of multilateralism. The rules-based system is best suited to India's needs, which is why the country is committed to it. It is the developing countries, more than anyone else, that need a successful conclusion to the Doha Development Round—the negotiation began in 2001 in Qatar to deliver development through lowering trade barriers around the world. Feeling that there was no negotiating space, I thought it best to leave.

In 2006, a picture was emerging of a significant rise in India's share of world trade, from 0.8 percent in 2003–2004 to (as was rightly anticipated) 1.5 percent in 2006–2007. This works out to a doubling of trade in only three years. The more the buzz of India's growth was heard in every sphere of the economy—whether exports of goods and services or imports—the more it was felt that it was time the rich countries were told that they could no longer think of India as a pushover. In that year, India's economic engagement with the world reached $447 billion (Rs 17.8 trillion), up by a record 64 percent from a level of $273 billion (Rs 10.9 trillion) in 2004–2005.

While the WTO had been set up in 1995, it was not the first attempt at establishing an international trade regime. Its predecessor,

GATT, was set up during 1947 and signed in 1948 with the goal of removing barriers to the free movement of goods. It became the platform for as many as eight "rounds" of multilateral trade negotiations between 1948 and 1994, and then, as part of the last round of negotiations, the Uruguay Round, the WTO was established.

The first three rounds of multilateral trade negotiations under GATT essentially focused on defining product coverage and placing caps on tariffs. The three rounds, thereafter, up to the Kennedy Round of 1964–1967, essentially revolved around reducing tariffs, and that too mainly on industrial products, thus quadrupling world trade. This continued in the Tokyo Round (1973–1979) as well. Significantly, in each of these rounds, the rich countries, mostly Japan and those in Europe and North America, struck trade deals exclusively with themselves in mind.

At that time, in the 1970s, most developing countries were still building up their industrial base. And, no developing countries had emerged, so to speak. The East Asian Tigers had not taken off, and the economies of Latin America, India, and China were still nowhere on the horizon. Naturally, GATT became a preserve of the rich. Trade was largely expanding strictly within the confines of what was then a rich nations' club. The rich nations got richer. The poor nations remained poor. There was nobody to speak on their behalf, nor did they have any clout on the international platforms. From the "rich nations' club" perspective, the low- and middle-income countries were "below trade"—that is, there was no comparison between the value of the rich countries' total transactions with the developing countries and the huge volumes of trade among the rich countries themselves. A diplomat friend, posted in Tokyo during my earlier stint as a minister (between 1991 and 1996), commented, "Why should Japan lower its trade barriers to India? How many Nikon cameras do we buy, and how many are sold in America?"

The glass partition between the rich and the poor nations was shattered in the 1980s, when China burst on the international trade scene. Then, beginning in the 1990s, it was India's turn to draw the attention of the world. At the Ministerial Conference in Doha, Qatar, the 142 WTO members agreed to launch a new round of trade negotiations. The intent of this round of negotiations was to make trade rules fairer for developing countries. It was different from the past rounds in its implicit recognition that China, India, and other developing countries were major trading nations.

One could, in fact, go further back in time. Three hundred years ago, India and China each generated a quarter of the world's wealth. Both lands were the dream of sailors, the aspiration of voyagers, the destination that every merchant craved. By the middle of the twentieth century, though, India and China together had plummeted to a miserable 9 percent of world GDP, even though they were home to almost 40 percent of the world's population.

Fortunately, destiny's hall has a swinging door, and, although China was the first to get through it, India was not too far behind. The result is the combined clout that the developing economies have lately earned; the Doha Round bears witness to it. This was only a beginning. But it surely was a new beginning.

What had made all this possible? In part, at least, it was due to the increasing global competitiveness of first China and now India. The rise of India did not stem from any outside aid or largesse. Indeed, several countries, particularly in Africa, that have been among the largest recipients of aid from the West are still struggling economically. If it is China's regimented labor and high productivity (although in an authoritarian milieu) that have led to its being respected, in India's case this respect has come from its demography, its human capital, and its potential for expansion of future markets, including trade in services, as well as its sheer competitiveness. In the pre-WTO world, trade was a game that "men" played while

India remained among the "boys," as it lacked the muscle, and the readiness, to compete with the world. Today it is a different story.

Just how different it is should be evident from the following facts. In the year ending March 2007, India's merchandise exports doubled, to $126 billion (Rs 5 trillion), from a mere $63 billion (Rs 2.5 trillion) three years before, when the Congress-led United Progressive Alliance government came to power. This is an annual compounded growth rate of 25 percent, compared to 12.73 percent in the previous three years. In 2006–2007, exports of IT services grew by 35 percent, ITES/business process outsourcing by 33.5 percent, and engineering services and products by 24 percent. These figures would have hardly seemed achievable 10 years ago. But now this is no longer just a dream.

Structural Flaws

Promoting free and fair trade between countries with varying levels of prosperity lies at the core of the Doha Development Round. And India is pivotal to this round by virtue of its size and the speed of its socioeconomic development. But leaving the two giants, India and China, aside, not much has happened since 2001 to carry the round's mission forward. Take Latin America, for instance. In the 1960s and 1970s, its per capita income grew at an average of 3.1 percent annually. Since the 1980s, the continent has embraced market capitalism, but its growth rate fell precipitously, to about an average of 1 percent. (In fact, the 1980s was the lost decade for Latin America, as if time stood still. Almost the entire continent was beset with a huge debt crisis and severe bouts of inflation.) However, the present decade is witnessing a change with greater macroeconomic stability and increasing growth rates. In Africa similarly, things have improved only marginally, with 20 percent of the continent having suffered zero per capita growth.

The WTO seems to have run up against a wall because of some serious distortions in trade, especially in agriculture, that the Doha Round is still grappling with. The most painful manifestation of these distortions is the enormous subsidies that the governments of the United States, the European Union, and the other developed countries are pumping into the accounts of their handful of farmers. In the 2003 Cancún talks, which collapsed in just four days, the growing global resentment against such a profound display of the rich nations' "wallet power" came to the fore with tragic effect when the South Korean farmers' leader, Lee Kyung Hae, committed suicide in protest against the refusal of the developed countries to recognize the multifunctionality of agriculture in developing countries. The Cancún meeting, which saw the European Union and the United States put up a joint defense on agriculture, also witnessed the emergence of the G-20, a group of developing countries led by India and Brazil. Since that time, the G-20 has transformed the tone of agriculture negotiations and emerged as the most dynamic force in putting the developed countries on the defensive.

The United States and the European governments have been disbursing subsidies to their farmers under multiple heads and in multiple guises. The beneficiaries of this largesse are very few in number, but the amounts involved are huge. In 2004, the latest year for which figures are available, the E.U. member countries paid out $36 billion in *direct* farm subsidies, half of which was swallowed up by the richest 7 percent of Europe's agricultural producers. In the United States, direct subsidies amounted to $23 billion in 2005. Of this, 72 percent was received by the top 10 percent of farmers. Moreover, there is a big subsidy for the export of agricultural products in addition to the direct subsidies. This can come in the garb of a humanitarian cause, like helping a poor country with food aid, or of environmental considerations—or often, without even a fig leaf of propriety. The OECD countries are now spending about $350 billion annually on agricultural subsidies.

To the rich countries, notably the United States, the right to subsidize agriculture appears to be sacred. But these subsidies have played havoc with developing countries like India, struggling as they are to fight agrarian poverty by raising farmers' income levels. Resource-poor farmers who are mired in poverty have no means to educate their children so that they can move into industry or services, or to improve their quality of life. Eking out a day-to-day existence is their first priority. The most dramatic manifestation of the harm that such subsidies can cause is cotton. The United States provides billions of dollars in subsidies to a few thousand cotton growers. This has devastated the livelihoods of millions of poor farmers in West Africa. In Hong Kong, I called this a "bleeding sore on the conscience of the world."

As the impasse in the Doha Round has established beyond doubt, agriculture still lies at the core of world trade. Some people may wonder why agriculture should pose such an insurmountable problem, amounting as it does to only 8.4 percent of world trade. But its absolute size is vast: $850 billion worldwide. More important, it touches on aspects of national identities. For example, Japan thinks that its people's cultural identity is defined by their eating a special variety of rice. The rider that goes with this is that no such rice grown outside Japan should be allowed entry into the island. This is also true of French wine and Dutch cheese, edible emblems of national identity. Chile may make a red wine as good as the ones made in Bordeaux, but France will not believe it, nor will it lower its tariff wall a finger's breadth to give the parvenu a chance.

Agriculture seems to represent the collective ego of the Western world. This is manifested in the subsidies that the taxpayers agree to give to farmers. The G-20 has urged developed countries to cut their tariffs on agricultural products by 54 percent. It has also called for a three-quarters reduction in U.S. farm subsidies. These countries have not accepted these recommendations. So far, the European Union has offered a 39 percent reduction in tariffs and the United States, a 53 percent cut in trade-distorting subsidies. Besides being inadequate, these commitments come with built-in legal escape routes, with exceptions, like nontrade distorting subsidies, packed into the many "colored boxes" that form the complex technical matrix of the negotiation. The agricultural subsidy issue, therefore, remains the heaviest millstone around the neck of the Doha Round, which was set to be concluded by December 2006. Since then, a year has gone by without any progress.

Fair Trade, Unfair Barriers

But subsidies are not the only way in which the dice are loaded against the developing countries. Through escalating tariffs, developed countries levy low duties on raw materials, which have low added value, and much higher duties on products with high added value. For example, while the import duty on raw leather in the United States is nil, the duty on a leather handbag is 20 percent. It is value addition that provides real gain, profit, and employment to workers in developing countries, and so it is always better to export finished products rather than raw materials. But as the value addition in a product line goes up, escalating import duties make it increasingly difficult for developing countries to sell these finished products in developed countries. The generally low average tariffs of the developed countries mask these tariff peaks, which are imposed on precisely those products that are of export interest to developing countries.

Nontariff barriers (NTBs) are even more pernicious. While the import duty on a product may be low, there are other requirements, such as labeling requirements, so-called environmental standards, labor standards, and a host of other opaque rules and conditions that render it all but impossible for small exporters from developing countries to penetrate the markets of developed countries. An example is the huge financial bond that U.S. customs authorities require some shrimp exporters from India to post on the off-chance that their product *might* attract antidumping duties. Leaving aside the legality of such a practice (which is now under question in the WTO), isn't the objective of this action to block small exporters? The prohibitive cost of the bond has made export uneconomical. The provision is akin to punishing an innocent person in the imagined anticipation that he *may* commit a crime in the future.

The other ring fence erected by rich countries involves dubious environmental standards; "phyto-sanitary conditions" is the trade jargon that stops Indian mangoes at the doors of the United States and Japan. The same mangoes, however, are perfectly fit for export to Europe and Canada. They have made nobody ill, nor have they devastated local horticultural crops. It seems that they become afflicted by a strange killer virus the moment they cross the land border between the United States and Canada.

India, for its part, has been opening itself to trade. India's average applied tariffs on industrial products have dropped from 126 percent in 1991 to less than 10 percent in 2007. Moreover, India's trade-to-GDP ratio is 54 percent, and the corresponding figures for the United States and Japan are 28 percent and 30 percent, respectively.

However, India certainly does not wish these autonomous tariff reduction efforts to now be used against its own interests. Some developed countries are calling for "real" market access, by which they mean reductions below the current applied rates, regardless of what the "bound" (i.e., permitted) rates are. (In the WTO, tariffs are bound, and the bound rates are those above which import duties will not rise. This is to provide predictability and transparency to WTO members.) Any tariff reduction formula—be it for industry or for agriculture—applies only to bound rates. This is a fundamental principle, and it is part of the mandate, as any other approach or baseline would not only mean shifting the goalposts while the game is in progress but also mean penalizing voluntary liberalization.

Developed countries are looking for "real" market access to developing countries. But India has already been providing such access, which is evident from the fact that its imports have been steadily increasing by an average of 30 percent every year for the past few years. India's imports last year were a whopping $190 billion (Rs 7.6 trillion); even if oil imports are excluded, the figure is about $130 billion (Rs 5.2 trillion). This is up from less than $30 billion (Rs 1.2 trillion) 12 years ago when the WTO was formed. If this is not real market access, then what is?

Service Charge

The Doha Round has included talks at various levels at Cancún (2003), Geneva (2004), Paris (2005), Hong Kong (2005), Geneva (2006), and Potsdam (2007). Amid the din of the battle over the main issue, agriculture, a muted subtext has been removal of the barriers to trade in services. The barrier that is the highest so far is that to the movement of people. In trade negotiators' parlance, this is called Mode 4 trade in services. India has made it abundantly clear in every forum that it respects national sensitivities concerning immigration. In any case, the government of India is not eager to encourage a brain drain. But there are protests even when Indian companies need to send their workers over to the United States on a purely temporary basis to integrate a software application or to perform some specific task. All hell breaks loose when some politician begins shouting about jobs getting "Bangalored."

The occasional screams that are heard in the West about the developing countries poaching on their services territory are rather superficial. The rich countries generally see the logic in importing services from, or outsourcing them to, the developing countries, as this makes their own businesses more competitive. Services hold the key to the Western economies. They account for nearly four-fifths of the U.S. economic output. The United States is also the world's largest services exporter, its income from this having reached $422 billion in 2006. Of course it wants entry into India's service market, especially as the range of services available for trading in the world is getting wider by the day. There is nothing wrong with that desire, provided it is matched with equal flexibility in other areas of the negotiations. There are about 160 service sectors/subsectors outlined by the WTO. We have opened up many of our services to foreign direct investment. But further commitments in services would require that the Western governments be less rigid on trade in general and on agriculture in particular.

The World Bank has estimated that removing all barriers to and subsidies for trade (including the barriers put up by the rich countries) would lift about 320 million people living on less than $2 a day out of poverty in 10 years. Some other economists put the figure at 440 million. Whatever the exact figure, it is indisputable that finding a satisfactory solution to the roadblock in trade talks involves the survival of a large number of people, a number that exceeds the total population of the European Union.

Nor can international policy on agriculture ignore the fundamental realities in three-fourths of the world. There are difficulties and concerns regarding the agricultural sector and the rural way of life in several developed countries, notably France, Switzerland, Norway, and Japan. But it is essential that the stark difference between the nature of the concerns in developed countries and of those in developing countries be appreciated. The standard of living may be a valid concern for farmers in developed countries; in developing ones, the issue is finding the next meal. Conserving the pastoral way of life or the rural landscape may be a legitimate concern in developed countries, but in developing ones, the concern is one of livelihood.

In India, more than 80 percent of the cultivators are small and marginal, with the average size of holdings being less than 2 hectares (4.9 acres). In Europe, the average farm size is 18 hectares (44.5

acres), and in the United States, it is 178 hectares (439.8 acres). The majority of cultivators in developing countries live on the edge of poverty, as cultivation is primarily rain-fed because the cost of setting up irrigation projects is so high as to be unaffordable. This makes agricultural incomes highly volatile and vulnerable to crop failure. This is not an India-specific situation. The story in Africa, Latin America, and the rest of Asia is the same.

All this would lead to the assumption that poor countries must subsidize their agricultural activities to a far greater extent than rich countries. And it would be rational to presume this. But the truth is that poor countries cannot afford to do so. The disparity between interventions by governments in developed countries and by those in developing countries is stark. It is estimated that the subsidies given by all OECD countries put together amount to a billion dollars a day, while a developing country like India is able to provide a mere $12 per annum per farmer in the form of minimum agricultural support.

What If It Fails?

After spending several sleepless nights negotiating endlessly—in Geneva, in London, in Paris, and in Hong Kong—I told my fellow ministers that I was a politician, not a mathematician. Bickering about numbers made no sense to me; what was more important was the *effect* of those numbers. During the negotiations for the Doha Round, there have been endless negotiations on how and to what extent tariff reductions by both developing and developed countries should take place. Various formulas with intricate computations have been put on the table.

Whatever the formula under consideration, India and the developing countries are committed to reducing tariffs on the basis of the agreements already reached. The most essential feature of the agreement so far is that for developing countries, there will be less than full reciprocity in all WTO agreements. This translates into the principle that while all countries will do something, developing countries are expected to do less than developed ones. This continues to remain India's and the developing countries' position. This was the basic premise of calling the ongoing Doha Round of WTO negotiations a "development round."

Much against the wish and desire of the developing world, if the Doha Round, a round needed much more by the developing world than anyone else, fails, then international trade will certainly not come to a grinding halt; but its repercussions cannot be measured by just a slowing rate of expansion. The repercussions would be far more profound. The poorest nations would be hit the hardest. They have neither a large basket to bargain with nor much market access to offer, and there will be no pressure on the developed countries to eliminate the distortions they have introduced in such key areas as agriculture. But the worst victim would be the WTO and its underlying premise of free and fair trade, as it would lose its credibility. Global negotiations would become passé. They would give way to bilateral trade agreements. That would turn the rationale of multilateral negotiations—negotiations that give a voice even to the weak and the marginal in the international community—on its head. And the world would not be the better for it.

Chapter 9

View from
the Outside

"Power will go to the hands of rascals, rogues

and freebooters. All Indian leaders will be of low

calibre and men of straw."

—WINSTON CHURCHILL,
on the eve of India's independence, 1947

"We stand on the ruins of an ancient city that

was the capital of an Indian kingdom thousands

of years ago. Today it is part of a modern Asian

city that is the capital of one of the world's great

nations. At the heart of a civilisation that helped give the world mathematics, cutting-edge businesses now give us the technology of tomorrow. In the birthplace of great religions, a billion souls of varied faiths now live side-by-side in freedom and peace. When you come to India in the 21st century, you're inspired by the past, and you can see the future."

—PRESIDENT GEORGE W. BUSH,
speaking at the Old Fort, Delhi, March 2006

These contrasting quotes are symptomatic of the transformation in the international opinion of India over the past 60 years. In its early years, India was seen as a poor, somewhat inward-looking country that was struggling to build a just, equitable, and democratic society. Today, it is seen as a country that is determinedly marching down the path of economic growth. It is lauded for its democracy and its adherence to both the rule of law and (in a wider context) the rules of the game. Yet India's transformation, much like the Indian economy and the quest for a just, fair, inclusive and egalitarian society, is a work in progress. As such, for many in the West— or indeed in other parts of the world—the attempt to slot, typecast, or categorize India remains a frustrating and unfathomable intellectual pursuit. In two generations, the Anglo-American political leadership has gone from deriding India as a nineteenth-century backwater to holding it up as a beacon for the twenty-first century. In one generation, ordinary people have seen the portrayal of India in news stories change from that of a food aid recipient to a producer of sophisticated software programs and high-tech goods.

True, other countries have undergone a similar transformation. In the 1950s, South Korea was regarded as a low-income, low-enterprise country. In three decades, it grew into an economic giant. The children of veterans of the Korean War were thronging shopping malls in the American heartland, looking to buy South

Korean televisions and refrigerators. Other countries have similar stories to tell. The differences in India's case are its scale and a commitment to democracy that runs simultaneously with a search for higher and faster GDP growth. When South Korea changed, it transformed a society; as India changes, it can transform the world.

The caveat here is that India's change is not an ordered, "one size fits all" change. It is not change by government decree, but rather it is driven by the energies of civil society, as it should be in a free-spirited democracy. This means two things. First, there are many Indias, and some of them are changing faster than others, depending on the capacities of individual segments of society to absorb and utilize change. Second, India does not—and cannot—hide its slow-changing elements; it will not banish its poverty to the countryside to create gleaming showpiece cities. If you visit Shanghai, you see Shanghai; if you visit Mumbai, you see India. In India, what you see is what India is.

This also means that media consumers or first-time visitors have to absorb many seemingly paradoxical pictures of India simultaneously. This tends to confuse them. Is this a poor country, or is it a middle-income country with a rich layer? Is it a country of cows on the streets or of IT wizards? Is it a country of roadside repair shops or of "intelligent factories" that produce sophisticated automobile components? Old India and new India, eternal India and dynamic India, yesterday's India and tomorrow's India, a predominantly Hindu India and a country with the world's second-largest Muslim population—or all of these and more. From the outside, India must seem a perplexing puzzle.

The Indian dialectic operates at all levels, including the outsider's historical perception of it. For generations, India has attracted the world's attention because of the supposed riches of its rulers. The man who discovered the land that is the mother of all the riches in today's world, America, got there by mistake, his real pursuit being a sea route to India, the land of bejeweled *maharajas* and their supposedly bottomless treasuries. But, historically, India has also been a land of religions based on renunciation. Another paradox to add to the complexity.

Gautama Buddha left his royal abode and family ties to become a mendicant and a spiritual wanderer until he founded, in the fifth century before Christ, the religion of enlightenment that later on became Buddhism. The Indian faith of Jainism pushes abstention to the border of starvation. In more modern times, Mahatma Gandhi glorified simplicity as a philosophy of public life and turned self-inflicted hunger into a potent weapon of political protest. This has now become his most imitated political act; the "hunger strike" is an accepted mode of protest at all levels of politics in India, from the national to the district. Which, then, is the correct picture of India? The land of unparalleled opulence and consumption or that of upholding sacrifice as a pillar of both private philosophy and public life?

The inability to categorize India under an identity rubric is often a problem of both space and time. Just as, as the old line goes, many centuries coexist in India (driving down an Indian highway, you can see bullock carts lumbering along on the shoulders while expensive SUVs whiz by on the main road), many regions of the world intersect in India. Is India then Central Asian? Certainly, the north of the country carries the stamp of Central Asia. Over the centuries, goods, merchandise, people, and culture have come down along the old trade routes through the land we know today as Afghanistan. Alternatively, is India a Southeast Asian country? If you travel to the southern peninsula and the eastern seaboard, you will be visiting harbors that once sent traders and merchant ships and migrants and cultural ambassadors to Sri Lanka and Bali and Cambodia. In parts of Assam, the largest state in India's northeast, the cuisine is similar to Thai cooking, using sticky rice, bamboo shoots, and even lemon grass. That again indicates an old intercourse and mode of economic exchange. Is India West Asian, part of the Greater Middle East? From Gujarat, the coastal state to India's west, flotillas of trading vessels have sailed down to Oman for generations. Indian businessmen set up shop in Aden, sold spices to the Arabs, and bought pearls in Basra. It is instructive that until 1966, rupees issued by the Reserve Bank of India were legal tender in Dubai.

As various parts of the Asian continent have influenced and interacted with India, some of this engagement may have been the result of war and religiocultural exchange. The substantial majority of it, however, was propelled by trade. Today, as the locus of global economic power moves back to Asia (where it had rested until the eighteenth century and the advent of European colonialism), India finds itself strategically placed to seize the moment. It is situated at the cusp of the various subregions of Asia, central and south, east and west, and it can be the focal point of a zone that is fast emerging as the world's politicoeconomic heavyweight. Every other part of Asia feels an empathy for India and has a sense of ownership of some aspect of India or its culture. In countries as diverse as Afghanistan, where India is now helping to build a national highway network, a power transmission system, and the physical and social infrastructure, and Vietnam, where it has set up an English-language training institute to facilitate that country's smoother integration into the ASEAN (Association of Southeast Asian Nations) economies, India evokes a certain comfort level.

As such, the geography that may so confound the Westerner works to India's advantage in its immediate neighborhood. The perception of India across Asia is that of a nonthreatening potential partner, a "gentle giant," as somebody once put it—never a predatory, territory-hungry nation. India does have territorial disputes with some of its neighbors, but it has not allowed these to get in the way of its desire for trade and civil exchange.

A Team Player

Indeed, not just in Asia but across the planet, India is seen as a nation that knows its limits and plays by the rules of the game. In trade circles, an unusual surge in a country's trade or its exports—in textiles, for instance—in a particular year often leads to suspicions of dumping or other unfair trade practices. India has rarely faced such accusations. Data from the World Trade Organization bear this out. In the period from July to December 2006, the WTO reported that China "remained the most frequent subject of the new investigations, with 36 initiations directed at its exports—up from 33 during the corresponding period of 2005." In contrast, India was "the subject of fewer than five initiations."

Scores of Indian companies are emerging as global players, looking outward with a newfound energy and confidence. In fiscal years 2005–2007, for instance, Indian companies raised $42.3 billion to acquire overseas companies, both big and small. Commenting on the "Marauding Maharajahs," *The Economist* noted in its March 29, 2007, issue:

> For proud Indians, nothing—except perhaps victory for their national cricket team—is as sweet as the sight of Indian companies marauding acquisitively across the globe. And marauding they are. So far this year Indian firms have announced 34 foreign takeovers worth more than $10.7 billion in all, according to Dealogic, a market-research outfit. Last year's total was $23 billion, more than five times the previous record and more than the investments made by foreigners in Indian companies.

Indian investment in many countries, such as those of the United Kingdom and Australia, exceeds the investment of those countries in India. Indian firms are actually becoming global, and the day is not far off when we will have a host of home-grown multinational companies operating all around the world.

There is a perceived dichotomy in India, permitting outward investment, and yet aggressively pursuing inward FDI. The reason for this is simple: foreign investment by Indian companies does in fact result in greater job creation in India. Indian ownership of companies that straddle countries increases trade between these countries, and trade creates thousands of direct and ancillary jobs. More important, this global acquisition results in the acquisition and transfer of modern technology. Technology is the key to industrial competitiveness. And industrial competitiveness creates still more jobs. It is interesting that these global merger and acquisition deals are not exclusively focused on the larger companies. As more midsized Indian companies go in for acquisition deals, the boost to India's economy will grow exponentially.

It is worth comparing the difference in the treatment of capital flows from India and those from China—or, for that matter, from Dubai. In 2006, Dubai Ports' attempt to invest in the United States raised a storm in Washington, D.C.; in 2005, when a Chinese company made a bid to buy UNOCAL, it became a high-voltage controversy across the United States, and China eventually dropped its bid. In contrast, Indian acquisitions abroad have been quiet and businesslike.

Indian companies have bought beverage and IT firms in the United States, coal mines in Indonesia, steel facilities in Britain, and aluminum behemoths in Canada. TCS, one of India's largest IT companies, employs 8,000 people in the United States and another 5,000 across a dozen locations in South America; Wipro has created approximately 5,000 jobs at its IT units in Europe and North and South America. Pharmaceutical giant Ranbaxy has 543 Americans on its rolls. In 2006 alone there were 40 individual deals of over $100 million (Rs 4 billion) in which Indian companies acquired firms or invested in the United States. In not one instance has a cultural disconnect or a suspicion of a politicostrategic motive been cited. Only in the case of the negotiations between an outstanding Indian-born, London-based steel magnate, Lakshmi Mittal, and the European steelmaker Arcelor did nationalism seem to become a factor, and even here the deal eventually went through in 2006. Likewise, when France's Lafarge buys Indian cement companies or Britain's Vodafone acquires a controlling stake in a large Indian telecom service provider, this is seen by Indians as quite normal, something to be welcomed and nothing to make a fuss about.

The fact that the very mention of the word *India* evokes no instinctive hostility, fear, anger, or even misgivings is important to remember when viewing and appreciating the new "personality" of India. It is going to shape the way the world will react to increased Indian capital flows and investments in other countries. It is a known fact that a national market can expect global participation only if its economy looks all right. It has to undergo a process of global "due diligence" before it can qualify for any higher level of engagement, much like the due diligence required when a company is up for acquisition: its books are subjected to the strictest scrutiny for any payable that sounds overgenerous or any receivable that is downright ambitious. Some countries—ambiguous on everything, from terrorism and nuclear intentions to adherence to good-neighborliness and democratic values—find it hard to pass this preengagement global scrutiny. In recent times, particularly since the 1991 reforms, India has not faced any problem on that score.

Part of the reason for the success of India's public diplomacy is that its story is seen as not one of government micromanagement and state-ordained economic policymaking, but rather of a billion individuals, all doing, if one can be permitted a colloquialism, "their own thing." If there is one thing that surprises Indians when they meet Westerners, it is the outsiders' astonishment at the fact that India is a democracy in a region where notions of popular sovereignty generally have not taken root. Indians take democracy as a given, knowing no other way of ruling themselves or even of living together. This relaxed sense of self is exuded outward, too. Other nations tend to trust a country that does not tell its people what to do, what to read, where to invest, and how to live and work. After all, India can hardly be transparent and open at home and opaque and scheming abroad. In that sense, the principles and ethical sources of domestic and foreign policy create a continuum.

Why are foreign perceptions of India, particularly those in less-developed countries such as India's old and dear friends in Africa and Southeast Asia, so important? It is not just because of the economic phenomenon called globalization or because of the need for mutually beneficial economic relationships. It is also because of the role that India can play in their development. Just over a century ago, in about the 1890s, the United States changed gears and began its acceleration towards economic superpowerdom. In 50 years, by World War II, this process had reached fruition. The American social and business model, its cultural levers, its institutional arrangements, and its self-identity as a nation became the template for the twentieth century.

India's rise may be analogous. It is the first democracy to aspire to become a strong economy, with planetwide reach, since the United States 100 years ago. The Indian experiment could become the prototype for the twenty-first century, the model for developing nations. What India's ascendancy represents to the world, then, is more than merely a competition for markets and trade and GDP numbers. It represents a contest of ideas, of the constant and relentless expansion of human freedoms: social, political, and economic.

The Diaspora Dividend

When the world sees, recognizes, and applauds India, does it actually see, recognize, and applaud *Indians*? Bill Gates, founder of Microsoft, put it best when he said, "It seems to me that the Indian miracle, if you will, demonstrates the wisdom of sustained investment in the primary asset of any modern economy—people." Part of the reason for the recognition of Indian talent has been the achievements of India's diaspora. There are over 20 million people of Indian origin living abroad, in places as far apart as Alaska and Azerbaijan. They own motels in the American Midwest; launch technology firms in California; make up one of the biggest doctors' associations in the United States; manage steel townships in Kazakhstan; run the public transport network in Santiago, Chile's capital; and teach at universities in Australia. The examples could go on.

In many ways, Indians are model immigrants. Industrious, hard working, and focused on merit-based and education-dependent advance, their human skills are much sought after. At a time when immigration and related issues tend to trigger convulsions, or at least strong debate, in Europe and the United States, Indians are being inspired to come over to work in these very nations. At one level, this is a tribute to India's prodigious human capital. At another, it is a salute to Indians as nonintrusive outsiders who settle into their host society, live by its rules, and add value to it, while enriching and enlightening themselves and their families. The Indian value system that migrant families cherish and seem to thrive on has added luster to the image of India itself. The 20 million children and grandchildren and great-grandchildren of India who live in over 100 countries around the world are really India's unofficial ambassadors.

Again one must here turn to history and to a search for precedents, if any. There have been, very broadly, two waves of economic migration from India in recent memory. The first took place in the nineteenth century and was forced upon unwilling peasant communities by the British rulers. They took "indentured labor" (a form of slavery, even if that term was rarely used) to Mauritius, South Africa, Fiji, or the West Indies. The descendants of those early plantation workers now form thriving communities. Some of the Caribbean-born Indians, such as writer-intellectual V. S. Naipaul, have won global renown and even the Nobel Prize. The second wave was a twentieth-century phenomenon that grew rapidly from about the 1960s; it involved the migration of Indian professionals and entrepreneurial talent to the West, and later to a whole host of countries spanning the continents.

Common to both of these sets of migrants is a cherished sense of being Indian, a commitment to their religious and cultural traditions and social heritage. There is no bitterness or strong negative feeling about "home"; these people were not pushed out of their native country by an inhospitable terrain, a famine or similar disaster, or a hostile government at the hands of which they feared persecution. As a result, even if the Indian diaspora misses the sights, sounds, and smells of India and even though it sometimes has strong opinions on the way the country is run (it is hard to meet an Indian who does not have an interest in politics), Indian expatriates don't meddle with politics back home in India. They don't advocate intervention by foreign governments; they don't carry historical baggage. They don't pull out all their investments from the country they work in and invest exclusively in factories and businesses or goods and services from India. Instead, they plow back much of what they have earned in the United States or Britain or even Dubai into start-ups and homes in their adopted countries.

This is particularly true of white-collar migrants. Indian software entrepreneurs set up companies in Silicon Valley before opening branch offices in Bangalore. The Indian mind has a singular rationality that allows it to separate the personal from the professional. An Indian can be true to both his *janmabhoomi* (land of birth) and his *karmabhoomi* (land of professional achievement). In a world that is increasingly defined by multiple identities and multiple senses of loyalty, this quality makes Indians respected and welcome.

And Finally, Democracy

"India celebrated the anniversary of independence by announcing new and stricter austerity measures. India is still basically a hungry land; the government has launched a drive to raise more food. To highlight the food drive, plows ripped through New Delhi's viceregal golf course. Governor General Chakravarti Rajagopalachari, no golfer himself, posed behind a team of bullocks."
— *TIME MAGAZINE*, August 22, 1949

"Sixty years after independence, India is beginning to deliver on its promise. Over the past few years, the world's biggest and rowdiest democracy has matched its political freedoms with economic ones, unleashing a torrent of growth and wealth creation that is transforming the lives of millions. India's economic clout is beginning to make itself felt on the international stage, as the nation retakes the place it held as a global trade giant long before colonial powers ever arrived there."
— *TIME MAGAZINE*, August 13, 2007

India is one of the very few newly independent postwar colonies to have stayed the course with democracy and, in fact, added to the democratic experience and the corpus of political science theory by innovations in multiparty power sharing, in federalism, in empowering people, and in fostering institutions that both underpin and build upon popular sovereignty. The realization that democracy in India is here to stay and is its natural mode of government and not a temporary aberration, has perhaps been an important change in how the world sees India. In the early years, there was an almost ghoulish wait for democracy in India to collapse and, as in so many other countries in Africa or Asia, for a dictator or military strongman to take over.

In 1967, as India prepared for its first general election after the death of Jawaharlal Nehru and after two wars—in 1962 with China and in 1965 with Pakistan—the London *Times* published a series of apocalyptic articles on "India's Disintegrating Democracy." "Famine is threatening," the Delhi correspondent of the venerable paper thundered, "the administration is strained and universally believed to be corrupt, the government and the governing party have lost public confidence and belief in themselves as well." He predicted a "readiness for the rejection of parliamentary democracy" and a future that was "not only dark but profoundly uncertain." As India prepared for its "fourth—and surely the last—general election . . . the great experiment of developing India within a democratic framework has failed." The breakup of India seemed imminent. Forty years later, there fortunately is still no sign of this.

Such prognoses were not limited to one newspaper or one era. In those early years—in fact, right up until the 1980s—there was a whole cottage industry of intellectuals in the West who cheerfully predicted that India was set to disintegrate or turn its back on democracy. It is a measure of how far India has come, and how much the world has revised its opinion, that such speculation is at an end. In the summer of 2004, Indians participated in the largest democratic exercise in human history: 670 million registered voters chose their representatives and their government. India had almost *double* the number of voters found in the United States, Western Europe, Australia, Canada, and Japan *combined*. The next general election will be even larger, with an electorate of three-fourths of a billion. In an age when nation building, social reengineering in far-flung countries, and the promotion and nurturing of democratic institutions in newly emergent nations are of profoundly compelling concern, India's adherence to its democratic timetable has won the admiration of other societies.

Yet democracy is more than just the holding of elections; to Indians, it is an article of faith. It can be argued that the British gave us the Westminster model of governance and elections, but it did not need to give us democracy. A democratic sensibility is part of the Indian ethos; it always has been. Indian citizens are not doing themselves a favor by being democratic; there is simply no other way of keeping the vast, diverse, and enormously varied nation together. When the world acknowledges India's democracy, it also bows to many other aspects of India. India is a stable society. Despite income inequalities, despite regional and religious pulls and pressures, and despite emotional and cultural passions, the pot never boils over. There is occasional turbulence, but it is largely confined to the ambit of civilized discourse.

This has become India's signature, and it tells us why, for instance, foreign investors are now choosing India above other likely business destinations. There is a sense of trust, credibility, and certitude that is absent in some other emerging markets. This too is a product of democracy. The process of voting—of walking into a voting booth, standing there alone with only your conscience for company, and making your political statement—is an almost sacred ritual. It is rewarding, and yet it is humbling. It makes all Indians, of all colors, castes, religious affiliations, educational backgrounds, and income profiles, equal. They are equal stakeholders in that larger enterprise called India.

The French novelist Romain Rolland once wrote, "If there is one place on the face of the earth where all dreams of living men have found a home from the very earliest days when man began the dream of existence, it is India." India's ethos is of one of the peaceful coexistence of people, of cultures, of ideas, of dreams. Not surprisingly, India's democracy has an extremely tempering quality. It forces candidates with angular rhetoric, ideas, and political platforms to eventually blunt their sharp edges, seek the middle ground, and reach out to the largest number—or face certain defeat on election day. It sublimates anger and frustration and disquiet among the people; by the mere act of voting, they can hit back at those who they think have done them wrong or let them down. India has a multitude of minorities. And the minorities coexist with respect for one another. This is not the result of some inexplicable alchemy. It is simply the magic of democracy. Minorities have equal rights and equal access to the voting booth. They have a legitimate outlet for their grievances, being bona fide citizens of India. They may have individual reasons to feel upset, but there is no overarching anger against the political system. It gives them their due voice.

The story of India's traditionally dispossessed caste groups—such as Dalits, once seen as "untouchable" by some—is similar. In 1997, as it acknowledged 50 years as a free nation, India elected a Dalit, K. R. Narayanan, as its president. He was born into a humble family, studied on scholarships, and rose to become an academic and a diplomat through sheer merit. Today, the chief justice of the Supreme Court of India is a Dalit; he has a similar, and similarly moving, life story. India's largest state, Uttar Pradesh, is ruled by a Dalit chief minister who built her party brick by brick and crafted a rainbow coalition that united the so-called upper and lower castes.

This is the power of democracy. This is the fertile social soil on which India's economy is flowering. This is the Indian miracle. Finally, the world is seeing it too. After all, as Lawrence Summers, former president of Harvard University, once put it, "Like people study political science, culture, public health, economics, law and medicine, students in Harvard will now study India as a subject." Rest assured that there will be no dearth of course material.

Chapter 10

The Obstacle Race

There is an irony in how the challenges facing India have changed. A few decades back, somehow getting the economy moving one step forward was challenging enough. It had been nearly stagnant for ages and would not respond to any effort at kick-starting. But now the problem is entirely different. It is maintaining the high-growth momentum that has already been achieved.

In the none-too-distant past, foreign exchange was so scarce that not a dollar could be spent unless it was necessary to save a life, or something similarly urgent. Now there is so much foreign exchange that the Indian currency has appreciated 10 percent in a single year. A problem of scarcity has turned into an issue of managing a foreign exchange reserve that is one-fourth the size of the GDP.

In the past, there were too many technically qualified people who were without jobs. Now there is a strain on the supply of talent for the quickly expanding industrial sector. Earlier, when the entire nation was seemingly reconciled to a cycle of low investment and low economic growth, even a spark of economic activity in any part of the country was most welcome. But now the centers of growth have mushroomed, although they haven't quite covered the entire country yet.

All this has only broadened the challenge, from having growth that would benefit just a few states, regions, and classes of people to having growth that is "inclusive," that is, benefiting all. Previously, the governments at the state level had not thought that it was their job to attract investments. They would seldom push for investment in a competitive manner. If people nonetheless invested in their states, it was considered to be due to *their* compulsion. But in India today, investors are a much favored people. With the state governments competing among themselves to lure investors in, a much-needed change is taking place. The vital connection between investment, growth, and popular votes is now understood. What has also been transformed—almost beyond recognition—is the profile of the voter. However, voters remain choosy consumers. As before, they expect their elected representative to deliver all that they need and all that they aspire to, but their needs and aspirations are very different from those of the past. This has changed the rules of the game of politics—and its basic challenge.

On the economic front, the big challenge is maintaining a sustained real GDP growth rate of 8 percent for at least a couple of decades. That is the precondition for India's entering the middle-income orbit. It was through two decades or more of high growth that the "miracle economies" of Asia, notably Japan, gained national and individual affluence. This effort calls for high rates of domestic savings and investments as well as high foreign direct investments. India is now witnessing a quantum leap in domestic investments. The current Indian growth story is a product of rising savings and rising investment, leading to rising incomes, which, in their turn, are making savings and investments rise still further.

The task ahead, therefore, is to keep the investments high from year to year. Hiccups in investments are likely if the agents that are involved (individuals, banks, mutual funds, and companies) make the mistake of putting too much of their money in speculative ventures, or projects whose future values are grossly exaggerated. This type of investment leads to what economists call "bubbles." But the strength of the Indian economy is that since 1991 it has been under a very strong monetary discipline, with the regulators ever alert to remove the minutest formation of froth from any corner of the economy.

But monetary control alone is not the sole guarantor of perpetually rising income, and therefore investment. If the state borrows too heavily in order to spend, this will push up interest rates, thus lowering the urge to invest. The most glaring problem in India's fiscal trends is the gross fiscal deficit, which, when measured for central and state governments combined, was 6.4 percent of the GDP in 2006–2007. India's gross fiscal deficit for the central government and the states together is among the largest in the world. The price a nation pays for high deficits is a high cost of capital, which, in turn, inhibits growth.

The Development Challenge

The larger the fiscal deficit gets, the smaller the state's capacity to make successful interventions in the economy for the general uplift of the people becomes. A large deficit limits the state's ability to alleviate poverty.

There is not and has never been a nation that didn't have its share of poor people. When observed over a long period, India seems to have been successful in managing poverty. Until the mid-1970s, the proportion of people below the poverty line (BPL) remained at more than half, with no declining trend. But this proportion dropped sharply in the late 1970s and 1980s—from 51 percent in 1977–1978 to 39 percent in 1987–1988. The poverty rate in 1993–1994 was measured at 36.2 percent. In 2006–2007, the government's National Sample Survey Organization (NSSO) came up with two different poverty rates, calculated using different methodologies. The two figures, 27.8 percent and 22 percent, are relatively far apart. However, even the higher figure is less than the undisputed figure of 1993–1994. So the poverty rate is certainly being reduced—quickly at times and not so quickly at other times.

Eradicating poverty must be a priority. India has an admirable record at *managing* poverty, with the benefits of poverty amelioration programs actually reaching the lowest strata, despite often-noticed problems of delivery. But it has had only a marginal impact on the aggregate numbers of the poor. In 1977–1978, when more than half of India's people lived in poverty, the total population of the country was around 650 million. Thus, about 330 million people could be counted as poor in that year. In 2006, the total population reached 1.12 billion. Therefore, the number of poor people was somewhere between 245 million and 310 million. Thus, although India's success in percentage terms is rather good, in absolute numbers it is less remarkable. It is because of India's uninterrupted poverty management programs that the country has been able to retain its social stability and avoid the unrest typical of poor countries, notably those in sub-Saharan Africa. But now it is time for the eradication of poverty, not just its management. Our government has enacted a new law that gives a minimum guarantee of employment to the extreme poor. This is not a program of just cash benefits but, instead, targets the creation of assets, with income to the workers as a parallel boon. Creation of such assets as essential infrastructure while managing poverty is a significant step forward in the endeavor to eradicate poverty.

Farm to Factory

Nearly three-quarters of India's poor live in villages. Rural areas are the ground on which the major battles against poverty are being waged. The absolute numbers of the poor have remained almost constant because of the low productivity of agricultural labor in India, and because of limited opportunities for nonfarm work in the villages. To give an idea of the difference in labor productivities between agricultural and nonagricultural work, let me give the example of my state, Madhya Pradesh. In 2001, while a nonfarm worker in the state could earn an average of Rs 80,000 ($2,000) a year in wages, the farm laborer's work fetched only Rs 13,900 ($348).

The productivity of agricultural labor in India is low for a combination of reasons. The pace of agricultural growth has slowed down since the second half of the 1990s, from 3.2 percent in the period from 1985–1986 to 1994–1995 to 1.7 percent in the period from 1995–1996 to 2002–2003. The declines in yield were largest in the states that had benefited from the Green Revolution of the 1970s; as such, though, the yields of many crops in India have been half those in comparable countries, including Vietnam.

The alleviation of poverty in India, therefore, is synonymous with bringing about fundamental changes in agricultural policy.

The agricultural strategy can no longer be focused on achieving self-sufficiency in food through high price supports, input subsidies, and highly regulated markets. Huge electricity subsidies to pump up subterranean water for irrigation of the fields crowd out more urgent subsidies for rural infrastructure, sanitation, and education of the village children. Overregulated markets, with laws that declare some crops to be "essential commodities" and thus restrict their movement to the best markets, have raised transaction costs, reduced competitiveness, and discouraged private investment. What is needed now is a holistic "rural life transformation" that changes the way people in the villages live and work. This is being done to an extent at the people's level, by increasing private investment in poultry, pisciculture, horticulture, cash crops, and dairy.

The strategy of the Green Revolution is no longer effective because the problems are of a different nature. There is, of course, a need for intensification, or yield increase, of existing crops. The stark fact is that China's groundnut yield, at 3,000 kilograms per hectare (2,676.5 pounds per acre), is three times more than that of India. Higher yields can come about through increasing cropping intensity, more irrigation, adoption of improved farm practices, minimizing losses, coping with water shortages by drip irrigation, and generating credit through warehouse receipts. It is also necessary for India to build on its existing strength in vegetables by concentrating on improving the quality of the crops.

There is also another aspect of rural poverty. It is an adjunct of the traditional rural life, which dissuades family members from looking for an occupation beyond tilling the few acres of ancestral land. As the family size multiplies over the years, the yield to each member becomes smaller and eventually becomes insignificant. Along with intensification and diversification, therefore, what is necessary is a well-thought-out exit policy from farming to non-agricultural activities. In India, such a movement is already happening, with the move largely being to low-value services, like construction labor and the transportation sector. But the challenge is to have people move to higher-value services—the services that information and communication technology (ICT) is making available.

Back to Basics

The condition of India's physical infrastructure requires urgent improvement. The country has one of the world's largest road networks, totaling 3.34 million kilometers (20,753,798 miles). But the quality of the roads leaves much to be desired. Many of them are narrow, potholed, or poorly asphalted. However, the 2 percent of the road network that forms the National Highways, measuring 66,590 kilometers (41,377.11 miles), carries 40 percent of the road traffic. But of this small part of the roads that witnesses most of the action, only 12 percent have four lanes; the rest have either two lanes or a single one. The good news is that modernizing 14,234 kilometers (8,844.6 miles) of the National Highways (including the Golden Quadrilateral linking the country's four major metropolitan cities and the diagonals between them) by giving them four to six lanes has already begun and is nearing completion. New projects to improve further stretches of the national highways, including creating expressways with full access control, have recently been initiated. Interestingly, the road improvement projects are being financed largely through a tax on petrol and diesel, thus bringing about a cultural change in India's socialist paradigm by making the road users pay for the new roads.

However, if the road deficit seems manageable, the deficit in electricity is more challenging. In 2003, India consumed 435 kilowatt-hours of electricity per capita, which was just about 40 percent of the consumption figure in China and about one-sixth of the world average. A generator is standard industrial equipment in India. Over 60 percent of Indian manufacturing firms own generator sets.

In the long run, the challenge of energy has to be met with nuclear power. However, in the short to medium term, India is also launching the coal-based Ultra Mega Power Projects, each with a capacity of 4,000 megawatts or more. Some of these giant plants are being put up in the coastal areas in order to make the use of imported coal easier. But many others will be pithead plants near the coal mines.

Whether the issue be roads, ports, airports, or energy, the crux of the problem of India's infrastructure lies not in accessing funds but in finding the right platform or vehicle for executing the project. Implementation of infrastructure projects involves two related but distinct issues: identifying who will *pay* for the new infrastructure and who will *finance* it. It is, of course, the responsibility of the citizens of India to pay for infrastructure, either through user fees or through taxes. In financing the project, though, the state has to bridge its "viability gap"—that is, the gap between the actual internal rate of return (IRR) of the project and the rate of return that is commercially viable. Ideally, there should be a special-purpose vehicle (SPV) made up of both representatives of the government and the private-sector participants, with the life of the SPV being limited to the project's full execution, including cost recovery. SPVs played a crucial role, for example, in the reconstruction of Europe's infrastructure after World War II. India has started facing the challenge of dealing with its infrastructure with a similar strategy.

Health of a Nation

The mixed blessing of India's large numbers is brought out most sharply by public health statistics. India has increased its life expectancy from less than 33 years at independence to more than 65 years today. Nevertheless, because of its size, it has what health economists call the largest "sick population," in terms of numbers, in the world. Officials at the United Nations Children's Fund (UNICEF) say that as many as 1 million children die in India each year of preventable diseases such as diarrhea, pneumonia, malaria, and neonatal illness. In many cases, simple measures such as access to potable water and an efficient sewage system could make a difference. Today, 46 percent of Indian children aged under three are malnourished; one in three malnourished children on Earth lives in India. Some 120 million Indians live with hypertension, and 40 million have diabetes. In two decades, these numbers are expected to increase to, respectively, 215 million and 70 million. Tobacco already claims close to a million lives a year.

At current levels, India's public health infrastructure is inadequate. It serves only one in five villages in the country. About 70 percent of all expenditures on health care in India is made directly by private individuals, without recourse to any form of insurance or social security net. Most Indians end up being dependent on private health-care providers. At the very top, these doctors and facilities are among the best in the world, even attracting a substantial number of "medical tourists," that is, Westerners coming to India for surgical and complex procedures at a fraction of the cost of these procedures in London or Chicago. Presently India treats 150,000 foreigners a year; CII (Confederation of Indian Industry) says that this will be a $1 billion (Rs 39.79 billion) business in 2012. But at the bottom, in the typical village or in poorer neighborhoods in big cities, the system leaves patients vulnerable to quacks or to incurring debt to pay medical bills.

These problems are most acute in India's north—in states such as Uttar Pradesh and Bihar, or even Madhya Pradesh, which I represent, where over half the children under three are malnourished. These states are among India's poorest regions; they are states in which economic change is slower, but also, crucially, states that are going to see large population growth in the coming decades and thus are going to drive India's demographic advantage. While the quantity of human capital is guaranteed, ensuring its *quality* is a challenge that India has to meet. Success is by no means inevitable.

In health as in other public utilities, the state is gradually giving way to the private sector. India has a constitutional commitment to the universal provision of health care, but the ratio of government to total expenditures on health is only 21 percent. This is half the public spending ratio in countries without even a token commitment to "socialism," such as the United States (45 percent) and Chile (44 percent). India has one of the most "privatized" health systems in the world, its ratio of public spending on health care being sixth from the bottom of 195 countries listed in the "World Health Report 2005."

Thus, public health is a challenge that India has to cope with through increased budget allocation. Related to it is the challenge of the supply of clean water and sanitation. Even in urban areas of India, the public water supply system is inadequate. In Colombo and Jakarta, both Asian cities, the public water supply is available for all 24 hours in a day. However, in India, the hours of supply are limited. In the cities to some extent, and in the villages to a very large extent, water supply is emerging as a private business.

The Learning Curve

The chief source of the agony of rural India is that it has too many people who are dependent on agriculture. However, moving the surplus agricultural workforce to better-paying jobs in industry and services depends on the efficient delivery of school education.

If physical health is one attribute of high-quality human capital, intellectual capacity is another. In this respect, the government's major initiative, Sarva Shiksha Abhiyan (Education for All), to expand enrollment and raise learning achievement is critical. There have been reports of a massive reduction in the number of children left out of schools, from 25 million in 2003 to around 13 million in 2005, and this is an indication of the success of the campaign. Education is in high demand and is also being privately marketed, not only in the towns and cities, but in rural areas as well. In urban areas, private school education has been strongly supplementing the state sector. In Kerala, a state with above 90 percent literacy, 68 percent of urban students go to private schools.

In the villages, education is the first step toward enabling large masses of the poor to exit from agriculture. Today, even a low-technology industry calls for at least a modicum of education. Its doors will remain firmly shut to anyone with a mere four years of school education. The IT sector is an example. India has recorded signal achievements in information technology as a result of the spread of higher education in the cities. Its prosperity, however, has been of little consequence to the undereducated village lad. The census report of 2001 shows that 58 percent of India's labor force is involved in agricultural work. This percentage must be brought down substantially.

India has challenges to meet in both primary and higher education. At the primary and secondary level, the country has 1.2 million rural schools, but only about half of the primary schools have toilets. This is often a deterrent to female education. Teacher absenteeism is high; a UNESCO report suggests that on any given day, one out of four teachers in a rural government school does not show up for work.

The challenges in higher education are equally serious. Less than 10 percent of Indians in the college-age group are actually enrolled in colleges and universities. The funding of higher education and professional institutions poses a dilemma. For most of free India's life, the state has underwritten expenditures on higher education, subsidizing student fees in universities, setting up the Indian Institutes of Technology and premier medical colleges, and so on. Over the past 15 years, the government's outlays on higher education have begun to decline in percentage terms, with a growing emphasis being placed on school education. This emphasis on education has happened at a time when the economy has expanded and has increased its appetite for trained human resources. For example, the Indian IT industry will face a potential shortage of half a million professionals by the second decade of the twenty-first century.

It is imperative that India's reservoir of human skills not be allowed to be depleted. The United Progressive Alliance government has spoken of gradually raising public spending on education to 6 percent of GDP and has introduced a small surtax on income tax that is being used solely to upgrade primary schools. The prime minister had set up the Knowledge Commission, composed of some of India's finest technocrats and educationists, to draw up a road map and suggest policy changes that would, to use Manmohan Singh's evocative words, "transform India from an information society to a knowledge society." To make this transformation to a knowledge society possible, a public-private partnership and an increasing role for the voluntary sector—particularly in the delivery of primary education to underserved areas—are necessary. Also essential is an expansion in the number of private technical institutions and general universities.

It is significant that the incentive for basic education has started increasing in many nonacademic professions. In Delhi, the local government now insists that people must have successfully completed a minimum of 10 years of school education to drive one of its large fleet of buses. The new kind of jobs in the organized retail sector, including back-end operations, involve recorded negotiations, subject knowledge, and paperwork. These too call for nine or ten years of school education. There is thus a new premium on education that was not there in the past, when low-end jobs were mostly manual.

The Curse of Carbon

Having once been India's environment and forest minister, I am tempted to begin with a caveat about the challenge of keeping environmental degradation within strict limits. The world's worst polluters are those who live in the richest countries. Until they set the example, it is difficult for poor countries to walk the tightrope between developing the economy and preserving the environment. The high-income countries emit 12.8 metric tons (14.1 tons) of carbon dioxide per capita per year. The average Indian emits just about 1 metric ton (1.1 tons). The new environmental orientation toward efficiency demands that a nation emit the least possible amount of extra carbon dioxide for every increase in output. But this raises costs.

I am not arguing that any nation, rich or poor, can ignore the environment, as climate knows no boundaries. But the current focus on carbon dioxide emissions has put the nations that have already industrialized at a historic advantage and those that are industrializing now, like India, at a historic disadvantage.

It is to India's credit, though, that in spite of this, its industry has shown considerable restraint in emissions. Its carbon dioxide emission per unit of GDP in purchasing power parity terms is 0.35, which is considerably lower than that of China (0.66), the OECD countries (0.44), and the United States (0.54). Despite India's low ranking in per capita ownership of emission-prone items like cars, the country seems to have accepted its environmental commitments. Incandescent lights are being phased out. The ongoing urban rapid transport projects, which cost billions of dollars, hold the bright promise of cutting back on the use of individual cars. There have been large fresh investments in developing India's hydroelectric potential. The Indo-U.S. nuclear agreement is a long-term insurance against emission from thermal plants. While India is trying hard to keep its emission of the greenhouse gases as low as possible, can't it rightfully expect that the rich of the world would refrain from letting their gas-guzzling SUVs hog so many miles every day and occasionally practice flicking the electric switch off, too?

Including the Excluded

India's recent successes have not been distributed equally. Some states have done much better than others. Even in the states that have prospered, there have been areas or districts that have outshone others. India's crucial challenge is to make growth more inclusive.

Just 7 poor states, out of a total of 25 states in India—Chattisgarh, Bihar, Jharkhand, Orissa, Madhya Pradesh, Rajasthan, and Uttar Pradesh—are home to nearly 50 percent of India's poor. World Bank studies have shown that the average per capita income of these 7 states has lagged behind that of 10 rich and large states by 29 percent in 1980–1981, and the lag increased to 46 percent in 1999–2000. These states are undoubtedly getting poorer in comparative terms.

In addition, since India is a country with a deep hinterland distant from the seaports, the wave of globalization in trade is pushing the coastal states to a position of advantage. The states of Gujarat and Maharashtra, which are blessed with long coastlines and good seaports, have been industrially advanced historically. Now the expansion of global trade has multiplied their competitiveness. It has put such states miles ahead of landlocked states like Bihar or Madhya Pradesh, even though those states have rich mineral and forest resources.

The positive sign is that competition to attract investment is increasing among these states. The proposed freight corridor between

Delhi and the port city of Mumbai will act as an equalizing agent, offering inclusive growth opportunities to landlocked states. It will also push up property values in the laggard states, thus bringing more investible capital to the table.

The challenge also involves including in the economic growth process the 85 million Indians known as members of the Scheduled Tribes (ST). About 10 million of them live in the northeastern states; because of their higher education levels, these people are better off than other tribals, who live along an arc of forests and hills in India's interiors. A lot needs to be done to effectively engage them in the process of democratic competition and economic development.

This is more than just a problem of inequality of income; it is a problem of democracy and education not being able to move deep enough into the lives of ethnic outliers. It is a challenge that must be met.

Managing Expectations

If J. R. D. Tata had wished to see India as the Asian tiger "uncaged," his desire would have been at least partly satisfied by the stupendous growth in the size of its economy. However, in per capita terms, India is of course more toward the bottom end. But there also it has given unmistakable signals of upward progression, from 163rd in 1999 to 144th in 2005. It has engaged with the global economy as never before, perhaps, with trade in goods and services accounting for over 37 percent of GDP in 2005 and about 54 percent in 2006. And, over all these years, it has stepped harder and harder on the gas, making the economy now grow at over 9 percent, which is three times as fast as the growth rate of the global economy.

It is an established fact, though, that one cannot expect a growth rate to rise at this swift rate forever. It must stabilize at a sustainable level, beyond which there may be constraints on either supply or demand, and the rate of growth may not just remain on a plateau but slope downward. This happened to Chile in the 1980s, Mexico in the 1990s, and most of East Asia in the latter half of the 1990s. It is the business of professional economists to decide what is the sustainable level of growth for India at this stage. It is clear, however, that whatever that level is, it is dynamic and can be raised still further by deepening and widening the reforms. And that's where the politician comes in. The economist can chart a course for reform, but implementing those reforms is the politician's job. It is also the politician's challenge. Liberalization is not only about freeing governance from the shackles of bureaucracy but also about offering an efficient, effective, and people-friendly administration. This calls for an attitudinal shift. We require reform of the government and public institutions, in addition to economic reforms.

Good governance and good policy cannot be separated from social sensitivity. In its modern history, at many stages—1947 and 1991 are just two examples—India has been offered the choice between adopting the economics-driven road or the people-driven one. Each time, it has chosen the people-driven approach. This situation is not going to change; it is a badge of honor and a must given the country's diversity and disparity. One cannot talk of India's growth without linking its economic achievement to its democracy and pluralism. Unless development touches the poorest of the poor people, globalization's dazzle and impressive GDP growth rates have little meaning. Unless the work inputs of the ordinary working people are visible in the enhanced purchasing power of their family members who are living deep in the dusty towns of India, no economic reformer can sleep peacefully at night with just new policy.

But I am optimistic about democracy and the way it works. When policy change goes through the welter of democracy, it may move slowly, but it emerges stronger and more sustainable. The challenge for a democracy like India's is to strike a balance between the possibilities of technology, the compulsions of the market, and the interests of the society and the nation. The ultimate challenge of politics is to make the greatest number see where their greatest good lies.

Chapter

11

Twenty Twenty

If there could be a real-life time traveler, the first passage he'd book would be to India in the 2020s. The country would by then have enjoyed almost 30 years of postreform growth. But that would be incidental. India's future cannot be extrapolated from its past. Rather, it is the present on which our vision of India in the 2020s must be based.

A bold idea, in fact, would be to land in the India of the 2020s after a quick tour of the rich nations—rich and old. It would be quite a spectacle: seeing the aging workers in some of the prominent cities of the West (retirement age would have reached 70 by 2020) demanding 24-hour weeks while many in India, one-third their age, would work 24/7 if required. The West would be sepulchral, metaphorically, and the East vibrant. In the West, the old would far outnumber the young. In the East, it would be the other way around. The Western economies would be feeling the pressure of pension liabilities, and yet retired people would remain unsatisfied. They might spend two hours every day at the sit-in at Trafalgar Square for more pensioners' rights. And with life actually beginning at 60, one might not be surprised if the discussions in Western Europe's parliaments centered on topics as profound as wrinkle care and memory loss.

Machines, especially those armed with some kind of artificial intelligence, would tend to rule over men. This is not to suggest that in New York's Central Park, electronic "dogs" airing their aged masters might be a common sight in the future.

It might, in fact, be a good idea to book a seat to India in advance. Getting a seat would not be easy, even after the arrival of Dreamliner Mark 4, seating 2,500 passengers. If the WTO could deliver by, say, 2010 a regime of free trade in services, India would soon emerge as the service emporium of the world. Most of the services would be IT-enabled, but some of them—the most valuable ones—would be delivered in situ. These would probably include high-level legal consultancy, complex surgical operations and post-operative care, book publishing, and the design of top-end products. One might imagine India in the 2020s being a combination of today's Vienna for its doctors, New York for its lawyers, and Milan for its designers.

Labor intensity is one of the key attributes of services, and education adds productivity to labor. And in absolute numbers, educated people are not in short supply in India. In 2004 there were 48.7 million college graduates in India, up from 20.5 million in 1991. The Indian government's renewed drive to boost higher education will lead to a doubling of the number of people graduating annually every five years, up from 2 million in 2004. Therefore, India would have a stock of 85 to 90 million graduates in the 2020s—20 million more than the entire population of France. Their education would include a good grounding in English. Obviously, very few countries would be able to match this number. It would be natural, therefore, for Indian legal, medical, and engineering consultancies to offer the best value for money. The abundance of highly trained professionals in India would also be of great help to, if not the last resort of, the beleaguered welfare services of the West, like the National Health Service in Britain and the social welfare systems in the United States.

To the global tourist, India's attraction in the 2020s would be multipronged, although its main charm would be the variety of services offered by its huge young, educated population. Such a tourist might come for hospital treatment organized by the medical insurer in the patient's own country. He or she might well be coming for legal help in drafting a contract or arbitrating a dispute. Or, of course, the person could be coming to discuss cutting-edge technology solutions. India's sterling asset would be its abundance of technically qualified persons with strong problem-solving capabilities, including the ability to deliver high-end engineering solutions.

Building on its human capital, India would play the role of a "technology magnet," as much of the innovation and production in the automotive and aviation sectors would have migrated or be migrating from the West to Asia. This shift would gather strength from India's established leadership in the engineering process outsourcing (EPO) business, which would have consolidated over the years. India would score in this area because transnational corporations (TNCs) would have been investing in their own R&D facilities in India. The TNCs' in-house offshoring of R&D to India would be an old story, as they had established as many as 150 captive R&D centers in the country as early as 2005.

In India, engineering skills grew mostly as an offshoot of domestic demand, with EPO being just a small part of the overall R&D story. It has been of great long-term benefit as far as the country is concerned, as specialized and superior skills were developed within domestic companies, both in the public and in the private sector. A public-sector maker of power generation equipment like Bharat Heavy Electricals Limited has very few equals in the world. For many years it has been a target for takeover by Euro-American giants. In the private sector, Reliance Industries Limited has for a long time managed oil refineries on a mind-boggling scale. Reliance has explored and recovered hydrocarbon fuels (oil and natural gas) from miles under the sea. In altogether different domains, it launched a huge retail network, is developing Special Economic Zones in different parts of the country, and bought U.S. patents by the dozens to fine-tune stem-cell research for the development of a new generation of medicines and enzymes. The Indian private sector also includes a global powerhouse like the Tata Group. The Group's Tata Steel produces the world's lowest-cost steel and owns Corus, the Anglo-Dutch steel manufacturer, which is the world's fifth-largest steel company. Tata Steel's sibling company, Tata Motors, is planning to launch, in 2008, the world's cheapest car.

All this has contributed to a knowledge base that has developed internally by institutions having long contacts with the best in the West. By the 2020s, India's front-line companies and the best of its learning institutions will be collaborating to make original contributions to science and technology. It would not be surprising if, in the 2020s, India and China were found to be dominating the field of research. Maybe, by an ironic twist of destiny, respected journals like *Science* and *Nature* might decide to shift their base to India. This would be quite a rational decision, as India would have the largest number of English-speaking science and technology graduates in any given year. There might be a tendency even among cultural products rooted in the West—like the *New York Times* newspaper—to shift their base, as India and China would offer the largest markets for the products they advertise.

Further, the inexorable flow of globalization would have transferred most value from Hollywood, the hub of the American entertainment industry, to countries like India, where special-effects talents would be plentiful and cheap. In the 2020s, old-timers would of course talk about *How Green Was My Valley*. But it would be digital animation that would conquer Hollywood more than ever before. The screen would increasingly be larger than life, loaded with flying superheroes, starships in combat, and crawling tyrannosaurs. Digitally animated movies like *Toy Story* and *The Incredibles* might well have been the prelude. The film industry would crave digital animators, effects specialists, and those film-making professionals who would have mastered computer-generated images and digital composition.

This change in taste has already been putting digital animation in the forefront; for example, when Steven Spielberg made his intensely political film *Munich*, its crucial bomb explosion scene was entirely animated. But the cost of these effects would inevitably lead to the transfer of such jobs from Hollywood to Bollywood. At a third of Hollywood's price, India would offer men and women capable of making anything from the wackiest of cartoons to the most touching effects. Maybe the Penelope Cruz and Leonardo di Caprio of the 2020s will give their interviews in Mumbai, their workplace, with time gradually turning Hollywood into one vast Sunset Boulevard.

A Nation at Work

If India should become the world's service emporium in the 2020s, it would also be the world's busiest workshop. Take, for example, automobiles. To go by the projections of the Society of Indian

Automobile Manufacturers, there will be 41.6 million passenger cars and SUVs and 174.1 million two-wheelers on the Indian roads in 2025.

Going by the McKinsey estimate, in 2025, the Indian middle class, with annual earnings in year 2000 rupees value between Rs 200,000 and Rs 1,000,000 ($5,026 and $25,132, respectively), will comprise 128 million households. With the rise in income and standard of living, India will emerge as one of the top two or three carmakers in the world in order to assuage its hunger for cars. Assuming that only about half the cars made in India would be for domestic consumption, one can imagine the mind-blowing number of cars the country would be making. Imagination has to be given free rein to work out how much steel these cars would consume (or will car bodies be made of plastic by then?), how much the tire industry would grow as a result, and how many more people would be employed as chauffeurs, garage mechanics, and gasoline pump and parking lot attendants. The potential of automobiles to create secondary employment is enormous.

The growing numbers of passenger cars, along with public vehicles and freight carriers, would herald a big change in our concept of transport fuels. A switch to biofuels might be inevitable. Extensive cultivation of biodiesel plants like the wonder plant called *jatropha* would reduce the nation's fuel import bill and lessen the pressure on the balance of payments. It would also make wasteland valuable, as jatropha grows on nonarable land. It would carry the capital, organization, and discipline of industry into the middle of the wilderness.

After the Iraq war of 2003, when oil prices surged to over $70 (Rs 2,785.3) a barrel and the fear that they would hit $100 (Rs 3,979) was perilously realistic, energy companies from Britain to Australia began investing in India in jatropha. It was seen as more cost-effective than other biofuel feedstocks. For instance, the cost of producing one barrel of oil from soybeans was estimated at over $120 (Rs 4,774.8), from corn at over $80 (Rs 3,183.2), from sugarcane at close to $50 (Rs 1,989.5), but from jatropha at just a little over $40 (Rs 1,591.6).

The quest for biofuels, particularly ethanol, would trigger a surge of capital, and technical capabilities into India's sugarcane agriculture. Brazil has a head start over India in biofuels even though India produces no less sugar. Brazil's reputation for producing ethanol, however, is based on the fact that it has long since accepted sugarcane as a fuel crop, not just as the raw material for sugar and alcohol. The tables might be reversed, however, as India too would find fuel in the fields, not just underneath them. Historically, the sugarcane-growing districts of India have not been particularly prosperous. The 2020s could witness a new era of real biofuel magnates. Significantly, this would bring about the empowerment of the poor people dwelling on the fringes of cultivated tracts, most of which had once been forests but which were partially denuded of tree cover. Biofuel could bring about a new deal for the most deprived sections of the population.

But there will be a lot more to India's agriculture in the 2020s than biofuel. In fact, agriculture is headed toward being the biggest turnaround story. Commencing in 2005, our government deliberated on the challenges of agriculture, a sector in which 650 million people are in a trap of low productivity, low income, small landholdings, and nonremunerative prices. Deprived of much-needed investment in irrigation, and any investment whatsoever in postharvest facilities (warehouses, cold chains, market access, port/airport access, packaging, processing, and so on), the agriculture GDP had grown barely 2.5 percent in, say, the 10 years prior to 2005. Worse still, India's yield of major crops had languished far behind that of China, not to mention the United States. For example, in 2005, India grew 3,284 kilograms (7,240 pounds) of rice on a hectare

(2.47 acres), whereas China grew 6,259 kilograms (13,798.7 pounds) and the United States 7,438 kilograms (16,398 pounds). The ratios were even worse in cash crops such as seed cotton, vegetables such as tomatoes, and other noncereals such as soybeans.

Although the reversal of India's agricultural fortunes will be spurred by huge public investments in the farm sector after 2007, it would still need favorable "trade winds" in the WTO for Indian farmers to see their efforts financially rewarded. Such a breakthrough might come with the implementation (say in 2016) of the Doha Development Round (2002–2008). This would involve the United States and the European Union agreeing to cut back substantially on their agricultural subsidies. That would mark the end of an era of injustice in which billions of farmers and their families in poor countries suffered in order to please a few thousand farmers in the rich world. With improved price yields, agriculture would attract investment on the scale required to take its efficiency to world standards. This additional yield would not necessarily lead to a rising demand for fertilizers, as consumer preferences would lead to some food being produced organically. India would be the winner again, as its fertilizer use per hectare remains the lowest among major countries.

Nevertheless, a new deal in world trade, signaled by a successful conclusion to the WTO's Doha Round, would lead to a paradigm shift in India's agriculture. The price of an eggplant or a tomato grown in India would be determined on the shelves of Sainsbury's and Wal-Mart, not in India's highly restricted village markets. The domestic market for agriculture would brighten with the new focus on food processing, packaging and storage, and disintermediation of the trade. Interestingly, the resurgence in agriculture would take place without the need for a larger amount of land under cultivation. All that would rise would be productivity.

In the first decade of the century, India has already become the second-largest producer of both fruits and vegetables in the world. It is also the second largest grower of cauliflower, onions, and cabbage. The subsequent decade could see diversification to create added value—like high-quality broccoli side by side with cauliflower, bell peppers in a riot of colors, or a variety of edible herbs—if only the produce could be shipped in full bloom to the markets in Europe, the United States, and Japan. By the 2020s, the availability of freight corridors and cold chains, and the frequency of air cargo flights, would demonstrate India's "flower power." If India sneezed, the flower auction market in Amsterdam would catch cold.

The twenty-first-century revolution in India's agriculture is unlikely to be pure green, like its predecessor in the 1970s. It could be "brown," with India's large concentration of biosecurity level 3 laboratories giving it the reputation of exporting poultry meat with the least risk of avian flu. The agricultural revolution could well be "white," too, with the country building on its reputation for being the world's largest milk producer since the beginning of the century. It would be all the more spectacular for a country as densely populated as India—its population density is roughly 11 times that of the United States and 2.5 times that of China—to take the leadership in agriculture.

High income in agriculture, with accompanying improvements in education, health, and—more important—aspiration, would lead to a big-time migration from agriculture-related professions to industry and services. This would be one of the most remarkable social engineering feats in human history. It is possible that by the 2020s, about 200 million people who would otherwise have remained in agricultural occupations will move to offices and factories. That would take India's "inclusive growth," the motto of my Congress party, to its decisive phase. Remember, it took Britain 180 years, from 1801 to 1981, to bring down the number of its agricultural populace by 3.6 million. It is possible that India will move 60 times more people out of agriculture in one-twelfth of the time.

By the 2020s, improvements in the agricultural sector would be complemented by marked improvements in infrastructure.

The India-U.S. nuclear agreement of 2005, nurtured with dogged persistence by the Indian government and the U.S. administration, gave the country a gilt-edged opportunity to look beyond non-renewable sources—coal, oil, and gas—for the bulk of its energy needs. It also could bring India close to gaining the expertise necessary to tap its almost limitless potential for the use of thorium as fuel for nuclear electricity. In 2025, India would have a generating capacity of 25,000 megawatts from its nuclear plants. The shortfall in the global supply of uranium for use as fuel would persist. However, if the technology to bombard the thorium nucleus were to develop on a commercial scale by the second decade of the century, the share of nuclear power in India's energy basket might reach a very high level. With India believed to have a quarter of the world's thorium reserves, it would not be surprising for India to export its surplus power to other countries. Quite literally, India would become the "lighthouse" of the world.

In electricity, India has a huge deficit. But this is not true of its roads, as the country has one of the world's largest road networks, 3.34 million kilometers (2,075,380 miles). The biggest problem with India's roads was that investment in strengthening, widening, upgrading, and maintaining them was very inadequate. The big change began after 2004–2005, with a steady upward climb in the domestic investment rate and a remarkable increase in investment in infrastructure. There would also be a spectacular improvement in its transportation milieu with the completion of the proposed freight corridor from Delhi to Mumbai, followed by a north-south corridor perpendicular to it. While the first phase of this project would require substantial domestic and foreign investment, the corridor would become a fast track for the movement of exportable goods produced deep in the hinterlands right into the holds of the ships berthed at the port.

I don't know how reliable economic forecasts are. Looking at them, I am often reminded of Sam Goldwyn, Hollywood's Mr.

Malaprop, who said: "Never forecast, particularly the future." Besides, the fortunes of nations can always be subject to a sudden turn. Before the Meiji era began in Japan in the nineteenth century, how many people could have predicted the imminent birth of an economic superpower? I still believe, though, that, in the 2020s, India's unique demography will be the determinant of its destiny. According to McKinsey & Co., India in 2025 will have 9.5 million elite households with an aggregate disposable income, in today's dollars, of $540 billion (Rs 21,487 trillion). That's actually more than the GDP of all but 15 of the world's largest economies today (2007). *Forbes* was ecstatic over 40 billionaires being spotted in India 60 years after its independence. I wonder what the magazine's spin would be if the number from India were to match that from quite a few G-7 nations.

The presence of so many high spenders at home would give India a major presence in the business of brands. It is possible that a large number of top brands would fall for the seductive spell of size of the Indian market, seeking a share of it. I don't rule out Ralph Lauren branding the Indian *dhoti* or sari, although it would be a challenging task, I admit, to beat Mahatma Gandhi in the art of making the *dhoti* a fashion statement.

It is more likely, though, that the Indians, who are big suppliers to existing brands already, would launch their own global brands. And why not? Of all the pieces of diamond jewelry sold anywhere, 11 out of 12 stones are cut and polished in India. There is a bit of Indian leather in every LV bag sold, perhaps. However, brand building has been made a very expensive exercise by monopolists, the best example being the famous legal battle between Microsoft and Netscape. But competition would weaken resistance by existing leaders. In areas like apparel and leather accessories, where India has abundant raw material and a sizable market, it could create global brands too.

But there is also the likelihood of India's using the merger and acquisition route to acquire global brands across the industry spectrum. It would be embarrassing, if not improper, for me to suggest the brands that we might acquire by the 2020s. But I see no reason why a telephone company with most of its subscribers in India would not let its brand be Indian too, just as Arcelor steel is owned by the Indian-born steelmaker L. N. Mittal. If McDonald's finds one day that it is selling more of its trademark buns in India with a sliver of potato between them, called McAloo Tikki, than with beef burgers in America, then it will be time for the shareholders to favor a change in the brand's nationality.

It could be a time for change in such revered temples of the rich world as the World Economic Forum (WEF), which has traditionally met annually at Davos, in the shadows of the Swiss Alps, to deliberate on how best to promote the world's economic well-being. With Europe's global market share being on a slimming diet throughout the century, an eminently practical move could be to shift the venue to a rotation among Asian cities like Mumbai and Shanghai. The captains of world industry in the 2020s who still missed their skiing breaks between the WEF sessions would be free to take a short flight to Kashmir if they wished to put on their ski boots anyway.

A Middle-Class Nation— an Aspiring Society

In 2006–2007, the National Sample Survey Organization estimated that 22 percent of the population of India was poor. The survey was based on people's recollection of their consumption of food and other items in the recent and not-so-recent past. Based on forecasts, it is doubtful that the absolute number of the poor in the 2020s will be much lower, although the poor then will be much less poor than those today. India is on a growth path that offers inclusive growth to everyone alike; as U.S. President John F. Kennedy said, "A rising tide lifts all boats."

A law enacted by our government guaranteeing employment to the extremely poor in the villages would have been by then immensely successful in eliminating dire poverty from the countryside. Similar work guarantee laws for the urban poor would give them the self-confidence they once lacked. The Indian middle class has never lacked confidence. It has never believed one had to be born rich in order to succeed. By the 2020s, this spirit would have trickled down to the poor as well. They would no longer doubt their ability to move to a higher class within their lifetime. Besides, with many members of the rural agriculturist families having taken jobs in industry and services, there would be a regular flow of remittances. In many rural homes, these remittances would be old-age security for parents.

According to the McKinsey forecast, some time around 2025, India will have a well-defined middle-class population of about 583 million people, or 41 percent of an estimated 1,429 million population. Their annual household earnings, in 2000 rupees, will range between Rs 200,000 and Rs 1 million ($5,044 and $25,220, respectively) in purchasing power parity terms. Based on this forecast, therefore, the income level of the middle class in the 2020s will be much higher than what was generally regarded as middle-class earnings in the past. And the same will be true of the incomes of the poor and the "aspirer" class, known as the "lower than middle class" in popular parlance.

In the lower-income tiers, the extensive growth of organized retail establishments, from 4 percent in the first decade to substantially more in the 2020s, would create a large variety of job opportunities for members of the rural population with basic education. Various activites, such as sourcing, sorting, grading, and warehousing of horticultural products and vegetables in rural areas have the potential to absorb an entire generation of rural literates in decent livelihoods. The growth of organized retail establishments would also boost urban employment, with the creation of thousands of jobs in both the front and the back end of retail operations.

These socioeconomic regroupings would not lead to any conflict whatsoever with the nation's basic values, which are strongly founded on its culture. But they would create a large number of young people who were hungry for education, opportunities, and entertainment. In school education, both primary and secondary, India would address its shortage of teachers by novel use of IT. There could be virtual classrooms, each covering many thousands of children in several locations. In higher education, IT would be supplemented by private-sector participation. Private investment in education would become "for profit." As private investment in education ceased to be strictly nonprofit, there would be a large inflow of capital into a service that everybody craved. Instead of 15 Indian Institutes of Technology, as in the first decade of the century, there would be many more in the 2020s, as the private sector would be encouraged to set up such advanced institutions of scientific and technological education. In the first 60 years of independence, one of the main roadblocks to higher education was the paucity of teachers. With the market for education being open and competitive, being a college teacher would become one of the most envied, and best paid, professions.

Better education for all implies higher productivity of labor. The spread of education also means the intersectoral movement of labor—from low-skilled to skilled farming, from agriculture to low-skilled industry, from low-skilled industry to high-skilled and high-value industry and to skilled services. Goldman Sachs has estimated that intersectoral labor allocation alone contributed at least 0.9 percent to GDP growth in the seven years between 1997 and 2004. Such movement up the ladder of skills would keep India's labor productivity at a high level. This, combined with a high productivity of capital through increased absorption of technology, would put the economy on a growth trend that would remain uninterrupted for 20 years by 2025. A 9 to 10 percent nominal GDP growth rate over the decades would enable India to double its per capita income every seven years or so. This would be a rare feat. Manmohan Singh brought out the new spirit of India in his characteristic subtle manner when he said, in his Independence Day (August 15) speech in 2004 after becoming prime minister: "I have no promises to make, but I have promises to keep."

The rising income of Indians, as it happened, would turn India into a closely watched country. It would be imitated, too. This happened with Japan in the 1960s, when judo classes sprang up in the back alleys of Western capitals and books on Japan sold fastest on the shelves of bookstores. The Indian method of yoga as an exercise and *pranayama* as a meditation tool have long been accepted by sections of Western society. By the 2020s, these might be put into Western school curricula. In Europe, America, and Japan, Indian herbal medicines might give allopathic medicines a run for their money. Free from side effects and subject to the patent regime, these medicines have the potential to get a fair share of the worldwide market.

In addition to the general income growth, the 2020s would also witness growth in information technology on an unprecedented scale. IT would move not only into every classroom but into every poor person's home as well. Broadband would be a great leveler. Being armed with a device that enables a person to be online with anyone in the world, however high and mighty, at virtually no cost, would rid the young minds in India of imagined complexes. They would feel in no way inferior to their peers in the West. Moreover, IT would eventually become a powerful instrument of democracy, giving politicians an opportunity to take something like instant referenda on policy issues. The mass power of IT, combined with the state's obligation for disclosure under the expanding Right to Information, would be a potent mix that would give the world's largest democracy a powerful dimension to the concept of rule by the consent of the majority. And that would prepare the country to claim the trophy of leadership in the twenty-first century.

Chapter 12

As for Me

Mark Twain's eulogy after his visit to India at the end of the nineteenth century describes this country in all its ancient glory:

> This is indeed India; the land of dreams and romance, of fabulous wealth and fabulous poverty, splendor and rags, of palaces and hovels, of famine and pestilence, of genii and giants and Aladdin lamps, of tigers and elephants, the cobra

in the jungle, the country of a hundred nations and hundred tongues, of a thousand religions and two million gods, cradle of the human race, birthplace of human speech, mother of history, grandmother of legend, great-grandmother of tradition, whose yesterdays bear date with the moldering antiquities of the rest of the nations—the one sole country under the sun that is endowed with an imperishable interest for alien prince and alien peasant, for lettered and ignorant, wise and fool, rich and poor, bond and free, the one land that all men desire to see, and having seen once, by even a glimpse, would not give that glimpse for all the shows of all the rest of the globe combined. Even now, after a lapse of a year, the delirium of those days in Bombay has not left me and I hope it never will.

This prolific storyteller, who did not "overtly teach or preach through fiction," saw India for what it represented in every age and time.

Our ancient civilization has always fascinated the world. But for me, the story of my India has been an exhilarating journey of experiencing and participating in events that in just over half a century transformed a country into a vibrant and significant democracy, claiming its rightful place among the nations of the world.

My odyssey began when, as a young MP, just three years into my first term in Parliament, I found myself walking among the giants of the era. There were the autocratic yet charming General Zia-ul-Haq, dictator of Pakistan; the enigmatic revolutionary hero Fidel Castro of Cuba (I made a point of being photographed with this legend); the humane and gentle King Hussein of Jordan; and the outspoken Lee Kuan Yew, prime minister of Singapore, to name but a few. In the Nonaligned Movement summit (NAM) in the early 1990s, I was part of a group that got talking to Lee Kuan Yew, a rare NAM leader who was committed to the free market, and who tried to steer his colleagues, fellow prime ministers, presidents, and potentates, in the direction of economic choices. It was a futile effort, as the world was not ready for it. Yet the fact that Lee was somehow different, with views that were quite unusual for the period, remained in my memory. "Here is a man," I remember telling a friend shortly after the NAM summit, "who speaks his mind."

I always wonder how much or how little the world has really changed. Pakistan has another general at its helm; another king, Abdullah II, is ruler of the ancient Hashemite Kingdom of Jordan; and Lee Kuan Yew's son, Lee Hsien Loong, is the present prime minister of Singapore. They continue to drive the destinies of their countries, while old Fidel goes on forever! In the past three years alone, I have engaged and interacted with over 150 heads of government and ministers. The faces of the leaders have sometimes kept changing, as have their names and temperaments, but the most palpable and profound change has been in their perceptions of India, its people, and its international presence.

This passage through time, from NAM to the Earth Summit to today, has been a phenomenal experience. Over that period, in the pursuit of my official duties and even at leisure, I have been in continuous interaction with international heads of state, ministers, and CEOs of industrial companies and NGOs.

My first interaction with Angela Merkel was at the start of a dynamic and meteoric rise in her political career, when she, like myself, was the minister for environment. We had together cogitated and strategized on how to make the Climate Change Treaty work. And then, when I met her more recently at Hanover and Davos, had herself assumed the role of Germany's first woman chancellor and *Forbes's* most powerful woman in 2007, I realized that her respect for India had risen as sharply as her own status in international politics.

I have been quite beguiled by the conundrum that India

presented to the nations at large, when leaders from Chancellor Helmut Kohl to Prime Minister John Major to President Bill Clinton were inclined to like India but did not know how to translate that liking into action. Today, in sharp contrast, personalities from Chancellor Merkel to Tony Blair and Gordon Brown, the former and present prime ministers of the United Kingdom, to the Italian Prime Minister Romano Prodi and Japan's Shinzo Abe emanate overt warmth toward India, a country that they want to like and know exactly how to do so!

When I was a young entrant into the political arena, the reality that was India was both stark and startling. India was, to put it colloquially, a basket case. It was a country that was looked down upon and even ridiculed for its poverty, population, polity, and burdensome identity, with a fragile government and an equally fragile system of governance. Since India had not changed much by then in the perceptions of the world, that was the picture of India when I first met some of the world's foremost leaders. That was the impression that my country left on many skeptical chief executives of nations, companies, and NGOs. Yet today I see that these leaders of the powerful international fraternity appreciatively perceive the new India.

Right through the 1980s and mid-1990s, I bemusedly witnessed world leaders arrive on occasional visits to India without any agenda and unsure of what this country had to offer them by way of interactive relationships. Now their visits are far more frequent; there is an almost constant stream of presidents, prime ministers, ministers, and CEOs, accompanied by large business delegations, who alight on Indian tarmacs with a smile, a gleam, and an extended hand, their itinerary and plans meticulously predetermined, for an engagement with India in every conceivable business field.

There is every reason to exult in the exceptional metamorphosis of this young democracy. I recall the late Lewis T. Preston, a man with an astute business sense, a highly successful Wall Street banker, on a visit to India in November 1992 as the World Bank president, shaking his head and remarking that "India would never make it"! This otherwise farsighted man, who had rightly linked social justice with economic efficiency, would perhaps have been amazed by the India of the new millennium. Was it shortsightedness, or was it his inability to decipher the essence of the Indian character, evolved over thousands of years—down, but never out?

As for me, the challenge of promoting India internationally has been a labor of love rather than the mere responsibility of the office I represented. "Brand India" is not just a product that could be quantified; it is a historically extraordinary country, an India that, in the words of Will Durant, gentle philosopher and unique writer, "was the mother of our race, Sanskrit the mother of Europe's languages. She was the mother of our philosophy, mother through the Arabs of much of our mathematics, mother through Buddha of the ideals embodied in Christianity, mother through village communities of self-government and democracy. Mother India is in many ways the mother of us all."

Presenting Brand India while dealing with a steady stream of visitors from all corners of the globe required subtlety and creative improvisation. Sometimes my efforts worked and sometimes they did not. I have been surprised and thrilled by the expressions of delight on the faces of Western dignitaries when they received miniature idols of Ganesha, a Hindu deity whose presence marks the auspicious beginning of every venture, while a visit to the National Gallery of Modern Arts is sufficient to light up some demeanors. Occasionally my efforts have gone wide of their intended mark. In Paris, I had occasion to present the Japanese trade minister with a box of mangoes to make a case for the entry of Indian mangoes into the Japanese market. I thought that he would carry it back to Japan, but a few days later, he sent a note: "We enjoyed the Indian mangoes. In Paris. Thanks."

For decades, the world had been seeing the face of a nation in economic turmoil. However, what they had failed to discern was the hunger for change, the will and skill of a hitherto underrated artistry, the sweat of honest labor, and the spirit and fire in the hearts of each successive generation of youth, eager to be a pulsating part of mainstream India. The West may have been surprised by this fervor, but not we Indians, as the country was reinventing itself to take on the ongoing challenges that confronted our youth. The people of India have shown time and again that India is an ocean of talent with mammoth potential. They would not let an opportunity slip by.

As the state entered a new millennium, its emerging demography revealed an incredible transformation, with millions of educated Indians in the working age group, and almost 55 percent of the population below the age of 25. The turn of the century unveiled the world's largest English-speaking workforce, with a level of technical talent that was immediately the envy of many nations.

One of the most recognizable traits of Indian youth today is their redoubtable potential to compete internationally, with no sense of inferiority or bias to handicap their abilities. This is why the urban young entrepreneurs of this country are thriving. As a mere schoolboy I had perceived that teenagers are motivated by a defining self-confidence, impelled by the inquisitiveness of natural extroverts. Recently, during a trip to the United Kingdom, I paid a visit to the Said Business School at Oxford University. Addressing the faculty and students there, I was extremely pleased to discover a large number of Indians among my listeners. I was further gratified by the response of these young compatriots; they were in the forefront, asking me questions with a palpable sense of equality. In fact, it was a delight to discover among them a young, aspiring businessman who belonged to my parliamentary constituency, Chhindwara. Seeing this confidence in my countrymen further strengthened my conviction that one should not bow down to alien pressures in the international debates, particularly those that are not conducive to our collective well-being.

Indian professionals have been much sought out by foreign companies, educational and research institutions, and even governments for consultancies and for engineering and medical practices. Indians have carved niches for themselves and built exclusive business empires, with pride of place in the respective countries in which they reside. Their presence has grown proportionately with time, and it remains, amazingly, a distinct factor in the socio-political-economic development of both the eastern and western hemispheres.

In my travels to foreign lands and in my interaction with this ubiquitous Indian fraternity, I have marveled at these people's capacity to play pivotal roles in their respective societies, if not becoming leaders of their adopted communities. This is not mere admiration for the Indians settled abroad, competing successfully in circumstances adverse to a natural genetic ethos, but the acknowledgment that the people of my India have the tenacity, the diligence, and the inherent ability to stand up and be counted with their peers, anywhere and everywhere.

The proverbial wheel of fortune is slowly and inevitably coming full circle as persons of Indian origin are becoming prominent in the fortunes of countries like the United States, Britain, the European countries, and a host of other nations. Indian-born professionals are on the boards of various state agencies and corporate empires, in governance, advisors to presidents, and sitting in the British Parliament as well as in the hitherto unfamiliar preserve of the House of Lords. They are among the research scientists who are constantly making a difference in the quality of life and are even critical for the National Aeronautics and Space Administration's (NASA's) never-ending exploration of the universe. However, while it is inextricably linked to the fortunes of its adopted countries, the Indian diaspora is proud of its origin.

My passage from the rustic precincts of an economically and socially backward India to the corridors of power and policy making

has been another singular experience. As India's minister for commerce and industry, driving toward growth in both investment and
trade while grappling with the challenges of a world multilateral
trading system, the WTO, I have found the journey to be a formi-
dable experience. In the past three years, I have spent more time at
these negotiating tables than anywhere else. I have had to live out
of a suitcase, traveling nonstop and meeting captains of industry,
fellow trade and economic ministers, interlocutors, and heads of
government. It has been three years on a roller coaster and three
years of ceaseless education. This period is perhaps aptly exemplified by Dickens, in the opening lines from his *Tale of Two Cities*:

> It was the best of times, it was the worst of times; it was
> the age of wisdom, it was the age of foolishness; it was the
> epoch of belief, it was the epoch of incredulity; it was
> the season of Light, it was the season of Darkness; it
> was the spring of hope, it was the winter of despair;
> we had everything before us, we had nothing before us; we
> were all going directly to Heaven, we were all going the
> other way.

The constant pulls and thrusts of negotiations left me experiencing a gamut of emotions as we struggled to sort out a system
that would be fair to all countries.

I perceive that every country—big or small; rich or poor; developed, developing, or underdeveloped—is slowly being integrated into the inevitable unity that trade must inculcate between
the manufacturer and the user, in a rather grand scheme that no
amount of peace talks could have been able to supplement. Every
nation, no matter how small its dimensions and population, has
become a prospective marketplace for industry, retail business, and
services thereby facilitating and fostering a relationship of mutual
dependence tied together with an organic bond of trade.

Life as a politician has become too full of the present to permit the indulgence of peeking into the past. Therefore, I rarely open the cupboard where memories lie stacked. However, I was provoked to do that in 2006, when the news of the death of the Nobel Laureate economist Milton Friedman came. I had studied economics in college, in an era when the standard textbooks in India were reverential toward central planning, and there was little mention of a rising laissez-faire economist from Chicago who advocated minimizing the role of governments in free markets. Nor did the world know that this economist would emerge as one of the few scholars who would alter the direction of economic thinking in the second half of the twentieth century. On the pages of one of my spiral notebooks, I had scrawled his words on India as an "emerging power" that was awakening from "slumber," something that he had seen "a long time back."

The rise of India was predictable after the reforms were initiated in 1991. The success that has evolved has become more and more tangible with time.

U.S. president George W. Bush, the leader of what is unarguably the most powerful nation on earth, came to India. His arrival heralded India's ascending status in the global hierarchy when he informed Prime Minister Manmohan Singh that he had come to Delhi because he *wanted* the nuclear deal for India. In response, the Indian prime minister accepted the truism that India was now important to the world.

Shaking hands with me, President Bush remarked that I appeared to be the one who was "creating problems" for his trade representative at the WTO and other economic forums—a candid reference to my strong stand on contentious trade issues that were heavily loaded in favor of the developed economies. "Not at all, Mr. President," I responded. "Your trade representative, Rob Portman, and I are very good friends." The president smiled and professed a genuine appreciation of India's democracy, both in policy and as a live and working institution. A partnership between the world's oldest democracy and its largest seems very natural, assuming a convergence of beliefs, a respect for mutually treasured values, and a shared vision for the future of the world.

The former British prime minister, Tony Blair, was deeply driven by the hope of a thriving India–U.K. partnership, as well as a successful conclusion to the Doha Round of talks.

The difference between the acerbic and sharp speech from Prime Minister Lee Kuan Yew in his heyday and the fulsome confidence that this retired, wise statesman expresses for India today is the visible aspect of India's transition from its past to modern India. India's unique achievements in the past three years have been numerous, and one of them is the successful bid for Arcelor by the Indian-born tycoon Lakshmi Mittal, in the face of fierce opposition and angst from France and Luxembourg, to emerge as the largest steel producer in the world. And how the wheel has turned full circle when powerful leaders of strong countries are more concerned by such takeovers than the company's shareholders! I feel that developed nations find this aspect of the new India rather hard to digest.

My meetings with the G4 and G6, the apex trade negotiating groups consisting of the United States, the European Union, Brazil, Australia, Japan, and India, to formulate essential policy decisions was an exercise in the art in verbal fencing. Who can gainsay the immense knowledge of Bob Zoellick, the former U.S. trade representative and presently the president of the World Bank, who never looked over his shoulder for assistance, or for reassurance, in his relentless approach to trade negotiations? Or who can unnerve in a negotiation Brazil's foreign and trade minister, Celso Amorim, a disciplined master of mediation skills with a vast variety of experiences? These talks have been intellectually inspiring and pleasingly taxing.

Peter Mandelson, the young British commissioner for trade at the European Union, is someone to whom the press has not always been charitable—I wonder why! I discovered this vociferous person to be a sharp and acute negotiator, besides being committed to his work, yet a man that one could trust. Nevertheless, he sometimes evoked mixed if not piquant reactions among his interlocutors. I suppose Peter will always be an example of an intellectual, and as such a weird genius, who terrifies the people around him.

Then there is the adroit Pascal Lamy, a well-decorated Frenchman whom I have seen wearing two hats, first as the E.U. trade commissioner, where he was more European than French, and now as the director general of the WTO, where, but for him, the current Doha Round would have been not merely dead but buried. Rob Portman, the U.S. congressman and former trade representative, a dexterous politician, added his many skills and personal charms to the negotiating table. Susan Schwab, the affable yet unrelenting present U.S. trade representative, sometimes was too rigid when she did not comprehend India's issues. She is a good friend with whom I wish I did not have to negotiate.

In these three years, a metamorphosis of unprecedented intensity has steadily charged and changed India. Along with the rest of the world, I have watched the unfolding of a reform process, begun one and a half decades ago, that has impelled India from a vulnerable and tenuous democracy to an almost impregnable nation of irreversible polity and policy. The rising stock of India's worth in the global hierarchy can be seen in the rapid influx of multidimensional business, investments, and trade into the country. As the world's largest democracy, India has always enjoyed a unique political legitimacy. With added economic clout, this legitimacy will only grow.

It has been a long journey for India. At the time of the country's independence, the moment of "a tryst with destiny," when these words were first carried by radio waves across a partly sleeping and partly awakening world, resonating with intense emotion, citizen's of India had overcome centuries of foreign invasions, followed by 200 years of colonial rule. The country had survived centuries of invasive influences, absorbing the best of the alien features into its own culture. Since then, India has stood the test of credibility, despite the overwhelming sense of negativity that initially greeted the fledgling democracy. The challenge before it was like adrenalin in any person's veins. And today India is integrated as the world's foremost and largest successful democracy, despite its dichotomy and diversity. The world's recognition and revaluation of India may have been slow, but it was India's destiny, waiting to happen.

Respect and even admiration for the country's burgeoning affluence has been hailed by people everywhere. This puts India in the departure lounge with a boarding pass in its hand. Being a late flyer, India has gained the advantage of boarding a new-generation aircraft that may fly higher and more quickly. Starting late has a bright side, too, after all.

India's capacity to assimilate, synthesize, and modernize is infinite—that, in fact, is the nation's genius. But even genius can be stymied. Is there any guarantee that this country's economic momentum will not falter? India has put itself on the radar screen of every investing entity in the world, and each of them recognizes the fact that it would be impossible to do business without India. There is an increasing acceptance of India as tomorrow's tiger. Its assets—both tangible and intangible—will play a crucial role in the way the world develops in the years to come. As I have said many times, "while India may be behind in the sprint, we will win the marathon, mark my words!"

As for me, I feel an immense pride in the people of my India for their faith, commitment, and evocation of respect and admiration from the world community. My India is a new India, and it's an exciting India. It's an India of breaching divides, of dreams, of courage and persistence, and of a growing pride. We have worked hard to arrive where we are now. To quote the Indian prime minister, "A road is made walking step by step," and India is marching onward. Yet the road ahead is a long and arduous one, and it will remain a long haul for each successive generation. However, a revival of belief in oneself was and will remain an important step in this journey, and as we march ahead, each success will be another boost in a rising ascendancy.

As for me, I have always made a distinction between achievement and fulfillment. As a minister, achievement has come to me through vast and varied experience at the national and international level, but the challenge has been to engender a convergence of achievement and fulfillment, and to watch with satisfaction and pride as India moves forward with a momentum of its own creation. This will be true fulfillment.

Notes

Introduction

2 "Sometimes these memories float back . . .": Bharat is the Sanskrit name for India.

Chapter 1

14 "You will be lucky not to lose . . .": A candidate's security deposit is forfeited if he fails to get at least a sixth of votes polled.

14 "I had had little exposure to or direct experience of . . .": By the prevailing yardstick (the poverty line had been calculated at 1973-1974 prices), this was two rupees a day in rural areas, and two rupees 80 paisa in towns and cities. The exchange rate was then 7.79 rupees to a dollar.

16 "The first signs of change came in the 1980s, when a sales outlet . . . ": Bajaj Auto, India's maker of two-wheelers and a major exporter.

24 "Entrepreneurship, in the Indian context, is not bound by the classical definition . . .": Joseph A. Schumpeter, *Capitalism, Socialism and Democracy* (New York: Harper, 1942).

24 "After the partition of 1947 . . .": The partition of India in 1947 led to the creation of two independent nations, India and Pakistan.

Chapter 2

35 "Future historians would put the average annual per capita rate of growth . . .": Bipan Chandra, "The Colonial Legacy," in Bimal

Jalan, ed., *The Indian Economy: Problems and Prospects* (Penguin Books India, 1992).

37 "The roads in the countryside are notably better. . .": Milton Friedman, "Indian Economic Planning," Center for Civil Society, India, 1963.

38 "His excitement at finding a demonstrable example of division of . . .": *An Inquiry into the Nature and Causes of the Wealth of Nations* (Edinburgh, 1776).

39 "Business barons such as J. R. D. Tata, G. D. Birla, and Sir Shri Ram . . .": This is not the same as what the media in 1991 described as an attempt by protectionist businessmen to scuttle the 1991 reform.

41 "To this, the Mahatma's wry rebuff was: 'Industrialize—and perish.'. . .": It is typical of India's syncretizing genius that, to this day, Gandhi is revered as the Father of the Nation and Visvesvaraya's birthday is officially observed as National Engineering Day.

42 "In 1980, when I was in Parliament for the first time . . .": Jagdish Bhagwati, "The Design of Indian Development," in I. J. Ahluwalia and I. M. D Little, eds., *India's Economic Reforms and Development: Essays for Manmohan Singh* (Oxford University Press, 1998), pp.23-39.

43 "The industrial licensing system operated in league with a host of other controls . . .": For example, the iron and steel controller could decide how much steel was to be allocated to a certain carmaker in a given year.

45 "Even if one is pessimistic, and allows a 15 per cent chance of failure through interference by the United States . . .": Quoted by S. Gopal, *Jawaharlal Nehru: A Biography*, vol. 2 (Harvard University Press, 1976).

Chapter 3

51 ". . . according to the World Gold Council . . .": According to GFMS, *Gold Survey*, 2007, India's gold consumption has been the highest in the world. In 2004 its consumption was 841 metric tons (927.2 tons), in 2005 it was 1,049 metric tons (1156.5 tons), and in 2006 it was 961 metric tons (1059.5 tons). Gold import figures for India have also been the highest; in 2004 it imported 647 metric tons (713 tons), in 2005 the figure was 807 metric tons (889.7 tons), and it was 739 metric tons (814.7 tons) in 2006.

53 "But the real problem was the short-term debt . . .": A bankers' acceptance is a pledge by a bank to pay a designated person a designated amount of

money on a designated date. In India's case, during 1990–1991, the State Bank of India had accepted too many BAs that it lacked the funds to pay.

53 "Apart from the symbolism of the gold transfer . . .": A 1.4 percent GDP growth rate may be par for the course in the West, but in the developing world, growth rates are higher; in the six years prior to 1991–1992, the "devil's year," the average GDP growth rate was 5.6 percent.

55 "Those who needed imports in order to export . . .": It was known as Exim-scrips.

56 "This, of course, posed a major threat to the protected citadels . . .": This Bombay Club is different from the better known and more widely written about Bombay Club of the early 1940s that advised the Indian National Congress on the economic policy it should pursue post-independence.

56 "A ringing rebuff to the cringing by the Bombay Club members . . .": J. R. D. Tata (1904–1993), chairman of Tata Sons, the holding company for the globally known Tata Group, for 50 years, was awarded Bharat Ratna, the highest civilian honor in India, in 1992. He was the first and so far the last businessman to be given this award.

57 "Big changes were foreseen . . .": Foreign debt was $23.5 billion in 1980–1981 but had risen to $64.3 billion in 1990–1991. This could well have been a contributing factor to the 1991 balance of payment crisis.

Chapter 4

65 "Conventional wisdom aside . . .": Marshall M. Boulton, "India's Problem Is Not Politics," *Foreign Affairs*, May/June, 1998.

68 "In this period it had five governments . . .": Atal Bihari Vajpayee.

70 "In the 1990s, India was right . . .": A term coined by Joseph Schumpeter in his work entitled "Capitalism, Socialism and Democracy" (1942) to denote a "process of industrial mutation that incessantly revolutionizes the *economic* structure from within, incessantly destroying the old one, incessantly creating a new one."

Chapter 5

81 "In the words of a popular British historian. . .": Niall Ferguson, *Empire: The Rise and Demise of the British World Order and the Lessons for Global Power* (New York: Basic Books, 2003).

89 "At that time, TCS, short for Tata Consultancy Services . . .": Rafiq Dossani, "Origin and Growth of the Software Industry in India" (Stanford University, 2005).

89 "Let the software professional . . .": Department of Telecommunications.

92 "This is despite new engineering colleges starting up in hundreds and the number of fresh engineering graduates . . .": Including degree and diploma holders and those with MCA degrees.

94 "The nineteenth-century German Indologist Friedrich Max Müller . . .": F. Max Müller, *India: What Can It Teach Us?*, 1883.

98 "Indians educated in the post-independence institutions of scientific learning . . .": Bengaluru houses the Indian Institute of Science and the headquarters of India's space program and defense aircraft manufacturing outfit.

Chapter 6

108 "India's film industry, Bollywood . . ." In 2002, Bollywood made 1,013 films and Hollywood 739. Bollywood sold 3.6 billion tickets and Hollywood 2.6 billion. But Bollywood earned $1.41 billion and Hollywood $51 billion. All figures are worldwide. The difference is due to high ticket prices in the West. The gap has begun narrowing with the fast spread of multiplex theatres in India, where ticket prices are higher, starting at $2.25 (at the official exchange rate).

109 "It was exactly as Adam Smith described . . ." Adam Smith, *An Inquiry into the Nature and Causes of the Wealth of Nations*, 1776.

111 "But, regardless of its future course . . ." The first college in India to teach Western medicine was set up in Kolkata (Calcutta) in 1835.

112 "John Kenneth Galbraith, in his much-acclaimed book . . ." J. K. Galbraith, "The Investment Balance," in *The Affluent Society*, 1958.

Chapter 7

119 "In the heart of Delhi . . .": In Udyog Bhawan, set apart from the Ministry of Commerce and Industry, are housed the ministries of textile, steel, heavy industry, and small-scale industry.

123 "It calls for, among other things . . .": In India, the fiscal year begins on April 1.

129 "The amendments to the Patent Act were promulgated . . .": A special provision allowed the government to apply a law with immediate but temporary effect prior to ratification by Parliament.

Chapter 8

140 "Cáncun, which saw the European Union and the United States put Up . . .": G-20 members: Argentina, Bolivia, Brazil, Chile, China, Cuba, Ecuador, Egypt, Guatemala, India, Indonesia, Mexico, Nigeria, Pakistan, Paraguay, Peru, Philippines, South Africa, Tanzania, Thailand, Uruguay, Venezuela, Zimbabwe.

143 "That stops Indian mangoes . . ." The restrictions by Japan are gradually being lifted, after prolonged negotiations.

144 "The barrier that is the highest so far is . . ." Mode 1 is business process outsourcing/engineering process outsourcing/knowledge process outsourcing and other such offshore services; Mode 2 is tourism; Mode 3 is investments, direct and portfolio.

Chapter 10

170 "Higher yields can come about through increasing cropping intensity . . ." In the state of West Bengal, cold storage receipts for potatoes are tradable.

Index

Sources

In this book, the facts and figures have been obtained from the following sources

Auto Components Manufacturer's Association, India
Cambridge Economic History of India
Census reports, Government of India
Center for Civil Society, India
Center for Monitoring Indian Economy
Central Statistical Organisation, Government of India
CII (Confederation of Indian Industry)
DGCIS (Directorate General of Commercial Intelligence and Statistics, India)
Economic survey, India
Engineering Export Promotion Council, India
European Commission Statistics
Federation of Indian Chambers of Commerce and Industry
Foreign Affairs
Goldman Sachs publications
IMF working paper
India science report
Indian Brand Equity Foundation
McKinsey & Co. publications
NASSCOM (National Association of Software and Services Companies)
National accounts statistics, India
National newspapers and magazines

National Sample Survey Organization
NCAER (National Council for Applied Economic Research)
Planning Commission, Government of India
PWC (PricewaterhouseCoopers)
RBI Quarterly Review data
Reserve Bank of India
RIS (Research and Information Systems for Developing Countries)
SEBI (Securities and Exchange Board of India)
Society of Indian Automobile Manufacturers, India
The Economist
World Bank documents and publications

Many other reports published by the state and the central government, India